DISCIPLESHIP
Quad

GUIDEBOOK, PART 2

Bob Rice,
Author and Designer

Kristina Scheerbaum,
Chief Researcher and Editor

STEUBENVILLE CONFERENCES

FRANCISCAN UNIVERSITY OF STEUBENVILLE

Published by   Franciscan University of Steubenville
1235 University Blvd
Steubenville, OH 43952
© 2021 by Franciscan University of Steubenville.
All rights reserved.

Scripture quotes taken from New American Bible Revised Edition, © 2011 Fireside Catholic Publishing.

Images © Adobe Stock Copyright Agent, Adobe Inc., 345 Park Ave, San Jose, CA 95110, USA.

"Missionary disciples accompany missionary disciples."
—Pope Francis, *The Joy of the Gospel*, no. 173

ABOUT THE DISCIPLESHIP QUAD GUIDEBOOK

Over 35 years ago, Greg Ogden discovered the powerful potential of "micro groups" while completing his Doctor of Ministry degree. Although he originally believed the way to make disciples was the one-on-one model demonstrated by Paul and Timothy in the New Testament, his advisor suggested that he consider a variety of other models. He did so, testing the micro group of 3-4 people, one-on-one discipleship, and small groups of 6-10. He discovered that the environment created with 3-4 people provided for a powerful "hothouse" of growth that was not present in the one-on-one model or a traditionally-sized small group. He documented all of this in his book, *Transforming Discipleship*.

The Discipleship Quad Process was created based on that model but is driven by new content that reflects the beauty and teaching of the Catholic Church. Numerous years of research and testing by a collaborative team went into the development of the Discipleship Quad Process. The Guidebook was written and designed by Dr. Bob Rice, Professor of Catechetics at Franciscan University of Steubenville. Kristina Scheerbaum, who served at the Steubenville Conferences for over a decade, was the Chief Researcher and Editor. Mark Joseph, Vice President for Outreach and Evangelization at Franciscan University, oversaw the project.

The Discipleship Quad Process is a means through which the Holy Spirit will help us fulfill the mission Jesus gave to St. Francis to "Rebuild my church"… one disciple at a time.

This Guidebook is part two of four. More information about the Discipleship Quad Process, can be found at steubenvilleconferences.com.

TABLE OF CONTENTS

FACILITATION SCHEDULE.................................. 1
MY WEEKLY SCHEDULE 3
WEEK 11: GOD AT THE CENTER.............................. 4
WEEK 12: PRAYER FROM THE HEART........................ 14
WEEK 13: SPIRITUAL CHECK-UP 30
WEEK 14: TRINITY IN LITURGY 44
WEEK 15: BREAD OF LIFE 56
WEEK 16: LIVING WORD 72
WEEK 17: JESUS, I TRUST IN YOU 88
WEEK 18: INTO THE ARMS OF MERCY 100
WEEK 19: THE HEALING POWER OF JESUS................... 116
WEEK 20: PART OF A BODY............................... 130
WEEK 21: "AND THEY WERE ALL OF ONE HEART..." 142

FACILITATION SCHEDULE

WE PLAN TO ROTATE FACILITATION EVERY _____.
(Week, Three Weeks, Month, etc.)

WEEK 11 _____

WEEK 12 _____

WEEK 13 _____

WEEK 14 _____

WEEK 15 _____

WEEK 16 _____

WEEK 17 _____

WEEK 18 _____

WEEK 19 _____

WEEK 20 _____

WEEK 21 _____

My Weekly Schedule

Write down when your Quad meets and create a plan of when you plan on doing the different parts of the lesson each day.

SUNDAY

MONDAY

TUESDAY

WEDNESDAY

THURSDAY

FRIDAY

SATURDAY

THIS WEEK I WILL ›

✝ PRAYER REQUESTS

_____

_____

_____

_____

WEEK 11

CHARACTERISTIC OF A DISCIPLE: PRAYER

Prayerful

2 — PRAYER

God at the Center

God should not be only part of your life, but at the heart of your life.

> Hear O Israel! The Lord is God, the Lord alone! Therefore you shall love the Lord, your God, with your whole heart, and with your whole being, and with your whole strength.
> – Deuteronomy 6:4-5

> Father, may we not set our hearts on the passing things of this life, but grant us the humility to center our lives on you, the source of all goodness and love. We ask this through Jesus Christ, our Lord, who lives and reigns with you and the Holy Spirit, God, forever and ever. Amen.

THE Daily BREAD

WEEK 11

Martha and Mary: **Luke 10:38-42**

A psalm of trust and humility: **Psalm 116**

God blesses the humble: **1 Peter 5:5-7**

Humility is the greatest gift to God: **Luke 18:9-14**

Having the attitude of a servant: **Luke 17:7-10**

Main Verse for the Week: **Deuteronomy 6:4-5**

FAITH SEEKING UNDERSTANDING

When I was younger, I remember seeing a rusty pick-up truck with a bumper sticker that read, "God is my co-pilot." At the time, I thought this sounded like a great idea! Having God as our co-pilot means that he will be there when we need advice or direction. It means that he will take over when we need to fall asleep. It means that if something goes wrong, he can jump in and give us assistance.

Many of us who believe in God might like to think of him in this way because it keeps us in the driver's seat. Our faith becomes something that "enhances" our lives, like an upgraded iPhone or cutting out carbs in our diet.

From a "Part" to the "Heart"

But God wants to be more than a co-pilot. The memorized verse for this week was considered by the Jewish people to be one of the most important in the scriptures. The book of Deuteronomy contained the last words of Moses to the Hebrews, and in it he told them, "Hear O Israel! The Lord is God, the Lord alone. You shall love the Lord, your God, with your whole heart, with your whole being, and with your whole strength." Moses commanded the Hebrews to teach these words to their children, recite them before they went to sleep and when they got up in the morning, and to write them upon the doorposts of their houses and gates. The Jews call this command the *Shema*, which is Hebrew for the first word of the verse: "hear."

This verse (and many others like it) shows that God does not desire to be a *part* of our lives but wants to be at the *heart* of our lives. This isn't a "power grab"; it is reality. Sometimes we can use the word "God" so much that we forget what the word means. Webster's dictionary defines God as "the supreme or ultimate reality" or "a person or thing of supreme value."

Letting God Be God

Why would I want the "supreme or ultimate reality" to only be my co-pilot? Wouldn't my life be better if I was *his* co-pilot? If I was playing basketball with Michael Jordan, I'd be trying to pass the ball to him, not expecting it to be the other way around.

What I find to be mind-blowing is that God is so humble that he accepts a co-pilot status if that is all we are willing to give him. He will even sit on the bench while we try our pathetic best to win the game. God can ask us to love him with our whole heart, being, and strength because he loves us with his whole heart, being, and strength!

As St. Paul wrote to the Corinthians, "Love is patient" (1 Corinthians 13:4). God isn't trying to take over our lives (although he has the power to do so if he wanted to). Rather, he would like us to *give* him our lives. Not just some of it. All of it. Because the truth is, if we don't give our lives to him, it means we are giving them to something—or someone—else (usually ourselves!). Nobody can love us or take care of us like God.

The Front Page for Prayer gets its look from *People Magazine*. Why *People?* Because prayer isn't about doing something, but loving *someone*. We pray to a community of persons, the Father, Son, and Holy Spirit.

GOD AT THE CENTER

1. What struck you from this reading?

2. In the "car" of your life, where do you normally put God? The back seat? The passenger's seat? The curb? What keeps you from putting God in the driver's seat?

SCRIPTURE

The first words of Jesus in the Gospel of Matthew are, "Repent, for the kingdom of heaven is at hand!" (Matthew 3:2). Later in that gospel, he provides numerous parables to explain what the kingdom of heaven is. Here are a few of them: **Matthew 13:31-50.**

3. Which of these parables spoke to your heart the most? Why?

4. Jesus proclaimed that the kingdom of heaven is not just something we experience when we die, but it is "at hand"—here and now. How have you seen this in your life?

faith INTO life

Do you want to put God at the center of your life? It is easier said than done. Self-worship is an addiction and can't be overcome by simply wishing it away. The first three of the 12 steps that are used for addiction recovery can be helpful.

1. *Admit you have a problem.* This is always where recovery begins. Some people think it is no problem having God as a consultant or "co-pilot" in their lives. They justify this by thinking that it is better than leaving him on the curb! We need to come to the realization that the best role for God in our lives is to have him as *the* God of our lives.

2. *Believe that a Greater Power can restore you.* As we come to realize that we want God to be at the center, we come to the awful realization that we *just can't do it*, even though we want to do it. Our pride and selfishness kick in like a reflex—we have spent too much of our lives centered on ourselves to allow ourselves to be centered on someone else. So, we must believe that God has the power to change us (spoiler alert: he does).

3. *Decide to turn your will and life over to God.* Victory in the spiritual life is different than victory in the physical life. Physical victory requires a fight; spiritual victory is about surrender. That is why growing in holiness can be counter-intuitive for many of us. We are used to "doing," not "being."

These steps are based in the virtue of humility, which is the most essential virtue we need to have in order to pray.

Lord, It Is Hard to Be Humble…

In a culture that prizes boasting and achievement, humility gets a bad rap. We also see many examples of false humility—like when someone risks their life to save another then says, "It was no big deal." Both of these seek the same thing: self-praise. The boaster praises himself. The falsely humble says things to elicit praise from others. And then there is the other extreme of humility: those who think of themselves as failures or worthless.

The best way to think of humility is to think of it as truth. St. Francis of Assisi, one of the humblest people who ever lived, said, "Who we are before God is all we are, and nothing more." Through the blood of Jesus Christ, we are adopted children of the Father. We have infinite value because of God's infinite love. This is nothing we deserve; it is a gift that will never be taken away, no matter what we do! We cannot earn this love. We just have to accept it.

From Martha to Mary

You might remember from the gospel of Luke when Jesus was at the house of Martha and Mary. Martha was upset because she was cleaning the kitchen by herself while her sister Mary sat at the feet of Jesus. When she complained, Jesus told her, "Mary has chosen the better part" (Luke 10:42). Martha thought she needed to finish her tasks before she could sit and listen to Jesus, when it actually was the other way around.

We can't put God first, spiritually, in our lives unless we physically put him first in our lives. This is why a recurring theme of prayer in the Bible is marked by the phrases, "early in the morning" or "before the dawn." You will never *find* time to pray; you have to *make* time. Prayer isn't an optional part of being a disciple of Jesus, just as spending time and talking to your spouse isn't an optional part of marriage. It is the whole point! It is about growing in love.

You have already seen the fruits of prayer in your life by being a part of your Discipleship Quad, reading these reflections, and praying over the scriptures. But you've only scratched the surface of what God has in store for you (and in the next session we will talk more about personal prayer).

The two most important things to help us to grow in a life of prayer are humility and consistency. If God is only a part of our lives, we only pray when we are in need. If God is at the heart, we realize that we are *always* in need—not of his power, but of his love—and we commit ourselves to consistently sit at his feet.

5. What stood out to you in the reading?

6. What was your perception of humility up to this point and how as it changed after these readings? How do you struggle with this virtue (for example: boasting, being falsely humble, thinking you have no value, etc.)?

FOR YOUR ✚ GATHERING

RECALL (20-30 minutes): Begin with the Scripture and the prayer from the Front Page of the week. Then the Quad shares with each other how their week was, with a particular emphasis on how they experienced God working in their life. How did everyone do on the "This Week I Will" challenge?

REFLECT (50-60 minutes): The Quad shares how he or she answered the six questions from the lesson, as well as any inspirations he or she received from "The Daily Bread" or their daily meditation on the main verse for the week.

RESOLVE (10-15 minutes): The facilitator says, "God desires more than our activity. He wants intimacy. Jesus became flesh so that he could 'love us with a human heart' (*Catechism,* 478). He invites us to let him into the center, into the foundation of our lives. One way of doing that is to surround ourselves with reminders of his presence and love. Just as a girl might have pictures of her boyfriend on her nightstand, the home screen of her phone, or in a locket around her neck, a disciple of Jesus Christ should have things in his or her life that reflect their love for God: a cross around the neck, listening to Christian music, a picture of a saint on their phone, or a picture of Jesus at work/school. **What is one new thing you can do this week that would remind you of God's constant presence and love so that you can be more mindful in centering your life on him?**"

Allow for a moment of silence and then discuss. Write down those resolutions on the "This Week I Will" part of the Front Page of the following week. Then the Quad shares what else they would like prayer for and writes those intentions down in the space provided.

The facilitator then introduces the topic for the next week. Then he or she says, "Let us take a moment to listen to the living Word of God," and reads the accompanying Scripture, followed by a moment of silent reflection. The session closes with the Quad saying the prayer for the next week together, followed by an Our Father and a Hail Mary.

Next week has a bonus section, Discipleship in Action!

THIS WEEK I WILL

✝ PRAYER REQUESTS

_____

_____

_____

WEEK 12

CHARACTERISTIC OF A DISCIPLE: PRAYER

Prayerful

2 — PRAYER

Prayer from the Heart

Prayer is a personal relationship with God.

"But seek first the kingdom of God and his righteousness, and all these things will be given you besides."
— Matthew 6:33

Come Holy Spirit! Help us to fall more deeply in love with you, the Father, and Jesus. Reveal to us the unhealthy attachments of our heart and purify our hearts so that we can offer pleasing worship to you. We ask this through Jesus Christ, our Lord. Amen.

THE *Daily* BREAD

WEEK 12

Persevering in prayer: **Luke 18:1-8**

A psalm of trust in God: **Psalm 27**

The effort of prayer: **Matthew 7:7-11**

When we put ourselves first, we "pray wrongly": **James 4:1-10**

God provides all we need: **Psalm 23**

Main Verse for the Week: **Matthew 6:33**

FAITH SEEKING UNDERSTANDING

What is prayer? It is a word many of us have heard all our lives, but few have taken the time to learn what it is really about. For many, it is "holy thinking" or asking God for help. Though that can be a part of prayer, the reality of prayer is much deeper.

Simply stated, prayer is our personal relationship with God. It is the barometer of our spiritual life. Are you praying on a regular consistent basis? Then you are growing closer to God. Are you only praying sporadically, or not at all? Then you are distancing yourself from him.

The *Catechism* beautifully states that "whether we realize it or not, prayer is the encounter of God's thirst with ours" (2561). God *desires* us and "thirsts" for a relationship with us. In our prayer, we satisfy not only our desires, but God's! This implies a kind of prayer that goes beyond making requests. It isn't meant to be transactional, but rather transformational.

Prayer in the Spirit

How does this happen? It happens through the Holy Spirit. St. Paul wrote, "The Spirit comes to the aid of our weakness; for we do not know how to pray as we ought, but the Spirit itself intercedes with inexpressible groanings" (Romans 8:26). Prayer is like learning a new language—our mouths were made for it but it doesn't come automatically. This is why the Spirit "speaks" for us in prayer. Since we don't know how to "speak God," God sent his Holy Spirit to dwell in us so we can!

The Holy Spirit helps us pray from the heart. In the language of Scripture, the heart isn't just an organ that pumps blood. It is the center of who we are, something deeper than our thoughts and our emotions. It is the place we encounter God.

The Blessing and the Battle

Prayer is a blessing we receive from God. He loves us, he calls to us, he thirsts for us. He sends himself into our hearts to speak his language so that we can draw closer to him.

However, it is also a battle that we fight. We have two principle enemies in this struggle. The first is the devil. When you wake up every day, God has a "to-do list" for you and at the top of the list is, "Spend time with me in prayer today." But the devil also has a "to-do list" and the top of that reads, "Whatever happens, don't waste your time in prayer today." The devil will throw everything at you to keep your focus from God.

The other enemy in this battle is ourselves. Our hearts can be hard. Praying from the heart is vulnerable—there's a lot of junk down there that we don't want to face. We can be afraid of what God will think when he sees us like that, or of what he will ask us to do if we truly surrender to him.

Perseverance and Trust

This is why the *Catechism* tells us about two important things we need in prayer. The first is perseverance. We should expect discouragement in this kind of deeper prayer. A person learning a new language won't immediately be fluent. But don't give up—the Holy Spirit is there to help!

The second is "filial trust," the trust of a child in a father. God is not "out to get us." He is *for* us. He will not abandon us or let us down. He desires what is best for us, and he is the only one who really knows what that is. We can trust him with our heart. This is also where the Holy Spirit comes to our aid: "For you did not receive a spirit of slavery to fall back into fear, but you received a spirit of adoption, through which we cry, 'Abba, Father!'" (Romans 8:15).

PRAYER FROM THE HEART

1. What struck you from the reading?

2. Which is more of a challenge for you: perseverance or filial trust?

SCRIPTURE

Jesus prayed. Take a moment to think about that. He was fully God, but also fully human. His human nature *needed* prayer. If he needed it, how much more so do we! The apostles noticed there was something different about the way Jesus prayed, and they asked him to teach them how to do it. This is what he taught: **Matthew 6:1-33.**

3. What inspired you while reading God's Word?

4. Jesus said that "where your treasure is, there also your heart will be" (Matthew 6:21). Where is your heart? What does it mean for you to "pray from the heart"?

faith INTO life

Jesus prayed. For some Jews, prayer was something they did to draw attention to themselves: making a big deal about how much money they donated, looking haggard so people would know they were fasting, etc. For Gentiles, they would pray to pagan gods with "babble" or "empty words." It was a common practice back then to try to gain a deity's approval by reciting a long list of compliments and praises, thinking the longer the prayer, the more effective it would be. The goal of both of these kinds of prayers was self-centered. It was about getting God (or the gods) to do something for *them*.

From Us to Him

In Jesus' teaching on prayer, he moved the focus from us to him. The Our Father prayer is a perfect example of this. For what should we pray? *His* name to be exalted. *His* kingdom to come. *His* will to be done. For what should we ask? Our daily bread. Mercy. Protection from evil. Not the material things with which our culture is often so obsessed. While the pagans worry about what they will eat, drink, and wear, we should trust in God's provision: "Your Father knows what you need before you ask him" (Matthew 6:8).

Our focus in prayer should not be on a long list of things about which we are concerned. This would be like treating God as if he was a kind of divine ATM; when you don't get what you want, you think that something must be broken. Instead, it is about building an intimate relationship. If you went on a date with someone, but all they did was talk about themselves, I doubt you'd go on a second one! I can look back at many times in my life when my prayer was "me-centered." It wasn't fruitful; it was frustrating. Asking God for help can certainly be a part of our prayer, but it shouldn't be at the heart of our prayer.

Forms of Prayer

The *Catechism* has an entire section devoted to helping us pray in the way that Jesus taught us. It explains that there are five forms of prayer, all of which are included in the Our Father:

- **Blessing and Adoration:** It might feel strange to say that we should "bless" God, but in this context, a blessing means that we give permission. We begin by giving God permission to come more deeply into our hearts. Adoration is the proper attitude we should have before God—he is the creator and we are the creatures; he is the Father and we are the children. These reflections and Scripture readings are a great way to give God permission to move in your heart and bring you to a place of adoring the King of Kings and the Lord of Lords.

- **Petition:** Jesus told us to "ask, seek, and knock." The first thing we pray for is mercy, without which we can't even communicate with God. Then we pray for God's will to be done. After that, we pray for our needs, the greatest of which is to grow in holiness!

- **Intercession:** This is when we pray for others.

- **Thanksgiving:** We recall all that God has done and rejoice with grateful hearts.

- **Praise:** Thanksgiving gives glory to God for what he has done; praise gives him glory for *who he is*. Even if we've had a bad day (month, year) and nothing seems to be going right, God is still glorious! Praise frees us from our own selfishness.

A healthy time of prayer includes a balance of all of these forms. However, this isn't meant to be a "formula." Consider it as advice on how to have a good relationship with God. Give him permission to be the Lord of your life. Adore him as a child would his or her Father, or as a bride would love her groom. Ask for what you need, especially for those things that can help you love him more. Bring forward the needs of others. Thank him for what he has already done. Praise him for who he is. If this is new to you, it might even help at first to try to dedicate a few minutes for each movement of prayer.

Seeking First the Kingdom

If our focus is on ourselves and on this world, that is all we will be able to think about. Those kinds of distractions often reveal to us what our "treasure" really is. The *Catechism* tells us:

> A distraction reveals to us what we are attached to, and this humble awareness before the Lord should awaken our preferential love for him and lead us resolutely to offer him our heart to be purified. Therein lies the battle, the choice of which master to serve (2729).

Ask for the grace to "seek first the kingdom of God and his righteousness," knowing that he will take care of the rest. This is when we should pray, "Come, Holy Spirit!" *Of course* we are attached to this world because we spend all of our time in it! Prayer frees us from the anxieties of this life and puts our attention—and our hearts—on a Father in heaven who loves us so much he gave his only Son and breathed his Spirit into our lives. The "prayer in secret" that Jesus talks about is a prayer of intimacy, just as the most intimate moments between spouses occur in private. Prayer is falling more deeply in love with Love himself.

5. What stood out to you in the reading?

6. What form of prayer do you pray least often?

The next page has a bonus section, Discipleship in Action!

DISCIPLESHIP IN ACTION

We occasionally add a "Discipleship in Action" section when we feel there is more to say than what is included in "Faith Into Life".

There is a stereotype that many people have regarding prayer. They think it is something entirely spiritual and interior. However, since we are "embodied souls" (as described by St. John Paul II) created as both body and spirit, there are physical things we need to have in order to allow our spiritual lives to thrive.

Time

One of those physical things is *time*. You will have to make time to pray. For most people that means you will have to sacrifice something. It might be sleep. It might be some social media. It might be rearranging your work schedule. Time is the oxygen for prayer. Without it, the fire of the Holy Spirit can never burn bright enough to make any difference in your life.

There is value in spending enough time in prayer that you have the opportunity to let your mind rest in God's presence. If you are just starting out with setting aside daily prayer time, consider starting with about 15-20 minutes each day. After doing this consistently for one or two weeks, increase your prayer by 15 minutes. A good goal for consistent daily prayer is about 30-60 minutes each day. St. Francis de Sales wrote, "Every one of us needs half an hour of prayer daily, except when we are busy—then we need an hour." When we think we don't have time to pray, it is actually a sign that we need to pray more.

For long-term spiritual growth, consistency is important. It is better to pray for less time but every day, rather than a longer amount of time every other day (or once a week). The goal is to daily make your heart present to God in prayer. In order to help you, we have added a "prayer tracker" at the bottom of "The Daily Bread" section for the upcoming lessons. It includes a place to write out how much time in daily prayer you are trying to do (the box by the watch) and a place to mark off each day you were able to do it. It looks like this:

But how do we spend more time in prayer? A friend of mine, Jim Beckman, wrote a book called, *God, Help Me: How to Grow in Prayer*. He proposed thinking of prayer in four movements in order to help structure (and expand) your time.

Acknowledge (7-10 minutes): Acknowledge God by giving him blessing and adoration. In this time, give God your attention by telling him that you give this prayer to him and ask him to open your heart so you can listen. Consider the attributes of God that strike your heart and thank him for being those things (e.g., a good Father, provider, protector).

Relate (7-10 minutes): Share with God what is on your heart and mind. Think of this time of prayer as answering the question of a friend: "How are you doing?" Share your heart with God and be honest with him as you would if you were sitting down to have a cup of coffee or tea (or your drink of preference) with a very good friend. This is also the time of prayer in which you petition God for your needs and pray for the needs of others in your life.

Receive (7-10 minutes): This is when we listen. Many find this to be the toughest part. We are usually pretty good at talking and sharing once we get the hang of it, but listening can be a bit more difficult! Prayerfully reading Scripture is one of the best ways to hear God, so this is a great place to read the Scriptures associated with the weekly lessons. But don't stop listening when you are finished reading. Close your eyes and allow the Spirit to reveal deeper meanings to you. Remember that God always works through peace, so you can be sure it is him speaking if you feel a peace in your heart.

Respond (7-10 minutes): Respond to what you have received from God in prayer that day (even if the only thing you felt like you received was simply time spent with God). This is where praise and thanksgiving can be done. Respond to all that God has done in your life by thanking him for what he has done and giving him praise for who he is. During this time of prayer, it is good to consider a resolution for the day based on what you read or considered in the Receive time. This could be simply a resolution to trust God more throughout the day or to be more generous with those in your daily life. Making a resolution at the end of the prayer time ensures that you are allowing prayer to change you and your life.

Space

The second physical thing necessary for prayer is *space*. *Where* you pray is important. One might argue that since God is everywhere you can pray anywhere, and there is some truth to that. But our human frailty requires surroundings that are conducive to prayer in order to draw closer to God. I have a chair in my home with a candle and crucifix next to it and some icons on the wall. This is my "prayer space", and it is far easier to pray there than at work or in my car. I also love to pray in an adoration chapel, though I can only make it there occasionally.

A friend of mine who lives in a small apartment shared that, since she doesn't have room to make a separate space for prayer, she does a few things to make the space more sacred when she prays. She dims the lights, sends an image of Jesus to her TV, lights a candle, and plays some chant music (so the noise from her neighbors is less distracting).

If *time* is like oxygen, then *space* is the kindling, the place where the fire burns. It is simply a comfortable and quiet place with visual things that draw your mind to God.

Baby Steps...

Our physical body responds better with incremental growth than drastic change. Someone who isn't in the practice of running would be better to go for a 5K than a marathon. The same is true for our spiritual lives—it is unhealthy to go to extremes. There is no need to jump from ten minutes a day to sixty, nor do you need to hire an architect to build a chapel next to your home. The challenge for next week is to give *slightly more* time and/or space for prayer. Perhaps you could...

- Add five to ten minutes of your daily prayer, using "acknowledge, relate, receive, respond" as a guide.

- Try praying earlier in the day when "your mind is less distracted" and see how that goes.

- Do something that enhances your "prayer space."

- Pray at a church, chapel, or other sacred space where you feel more drawn to God (this includes nature, "the great book of creation," *Catechism,* 2705).

If you are not in the habit of daily prayer, or if you don't have a good prayer space where you live, that is the best place to start!

FOR YOUR ✝ GATHERING

RECALL (20-30 minutes): Begin with the Scripture and the prayer from the Front Page of the week. Then the Quad shares with each other how their week was, with a particular emphasis on how they experienced God working in their life. How did everyone do on the "This Week I Will" challenge?

REFLECT (50-60 minutes): The Quad shares how he or she answered the six questions from the lesson, as well as any inspirations he or she received from "The Daily Bread" or their daily meditation on the main verse for the week.

RESOLVE (10-15 minutes): The facilitator says, "Our readings reflected on what we need to have a deeper, more personal relationship with God, and the focus was on specific, intimate times of personal prayer. The *Catechism* tells us, "we cannot pray 'at all times' if we do not pray at specific times, consciously willing it" (2697). The interior dispositions we need are humility, perseverance, and filial trust, and our exterior needs are setting aside time and having a space conducive to prayer. **This week's challenge, as explained in Discipleship in Action, is to do *slightly more*.** As we share with each other what our personal prayer times look like and how we plan to respond to this challenge, remember this isn't a competition and there is no need for comparison. We are all at different places in our spiritual journey. Wherever that is, God is inviting us to take another step."

Share with each other how you plan to grow in prayer this week and write down those resolutions on the "This Week I Will" part of the Front Page of the following week. Then the Quad shares what else they would like prayer for and writes those intentions down in the space provided.

The facilitator then introduces the topic for the next week. Then he or she says, "Let us take a moment to listen to the living Word of God," and reads the accompanying Scripture, followed by a moment of silent reflection.

The session closes with the Quad saying the prayer for the next week together, followed an Our Father and a Hail Mary.

Additional Readings

In addition to Jim Beckman's *God, Help Me: How to Grow in Prayer,* here are my personal recommendations on what you can read to learn more about prayer:

Catechism of the Catholic Church: I would strongly encourage you to read the entire fourth section, "Christian Prayer" that begins on 2558 and ends on 2865. It is, in my opinion, the clearest, simplest, and most beautiful thing you can read about how to pray, and it has the authority of the Church behind it!

Abandonment to Divine Providence by Jean-Pierre de Caussade: Other than the Bible, I'm not sure I've read another book more than I have this one. In it, Caussade writes about how to live in the "sacrament of the present moment" and how the greatest prayer we can pray is continual abandonment to God's perfect plan for our lives. It is broken into very small sections that make it great for daily prayer.

Appointment with God by Fr. Michael Scanlan, TOR: Fr. Mike was a former president of Franciscan University, and he wrote this simple, short, and beautiful book about how to make time for God. You can only get our University bookstore at store.franciscan.edu.

Fulfillment of All Desire by Ralph Martin: It is a long book, but well worth the read. In it, Martin examines five of the great spiritual masters, all "Doctors of the Church": Sts. Teresa of Avila, John of the Cross, Catherine of Siena, Bernard of Clairvaux, and Francis de Sales. He beautifully weaves their teachings together to show how they are united in message and can speak to us today. My prayer life *exploded* (in a good way) after reading the wisdom contained in this book. Much of what you read in this Guidebook was inspired by it!

THIS WEEK I WILL >

✝ PRAYER REQUESTS

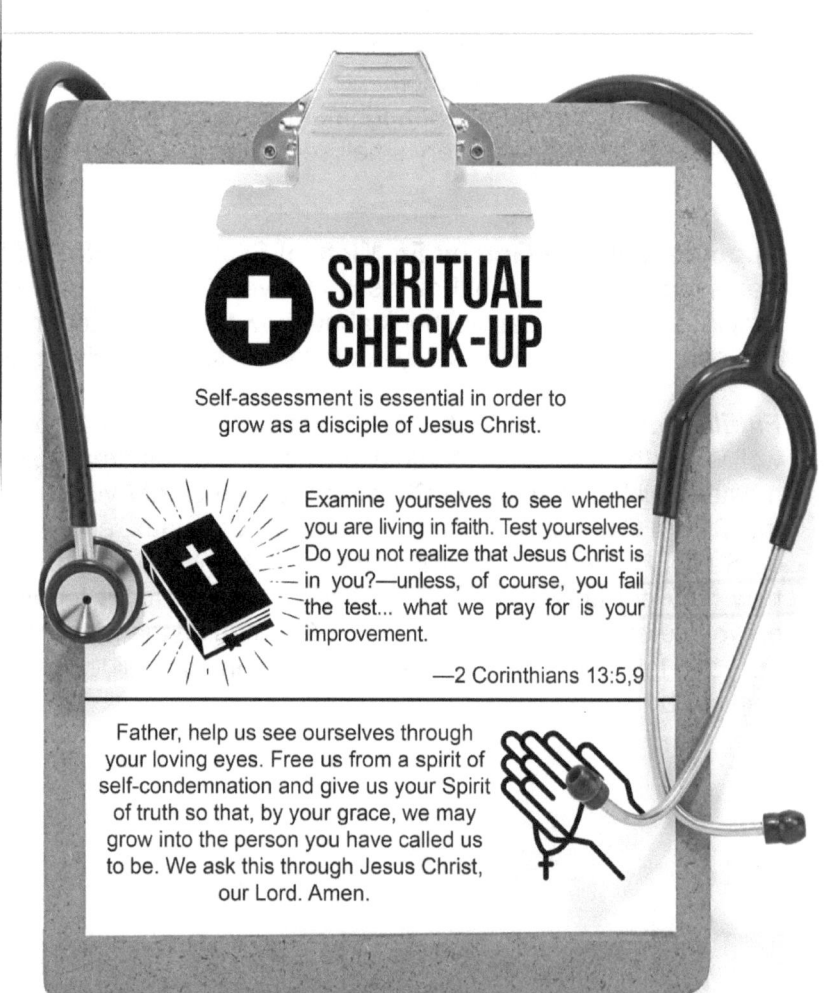

_____

_____

_____

WEEK 13

✚ SPIRITUAL CHECK-UP

Self-assessment is essential in order to grow as a disciple of Jesus Christ.

> Examine yourselves to see whether you are living in faith. Test yourselves. Do you not realize that Jesus Christ is in you?—unless, of course, you fail the test... what we pray for is your improvement.
>
> —2 Corinthians 13:5,9

Father, help us see ourselves through your loving eyes. Free us from a spirit of self-condemnation and give us your Spirit of truth so that, by your grace, we may grow into the person you have called us to be. We ask this through Jesus Christ, our Lord. Amen.

WEEK 13

THE *Daily* BREAD

Allow God to renew your mind: **Romans 12:2-3**

It takes intelligence to understand our hearts: **Proverbs 20:5**

Focus on yourself, not others: **Matthew 7:1-5**

Measure by God's standards, not our own: **Proverbs 21:2-3**

God knows us better than we know ourselves: **Psalm 139:1-6**

Main Verse for the Week: **2 Corinthians 13:5,9**

1 2 3 4 5 6 7

FAITH SEEKING UNDERSTANDING

St. Theresa of Avila, in her wonderful book *Interior Castle,* wrote, "Self-knowledge is so important that, even if you were raised right up to the heavens, I should like you never to relax your cultivation of it." She describes a soul progressing toward God as one who "will try to advance in the service of Our Lord and in self-knowledge."

She is not alone in this. A famous prayer of St. Augustine is, "Grant, O Lord, that I may know myself that I may know thee." All of the great spiritual writers emphasize that it is not only important to know God but also understand ourselves. This isn't an exercise in narcissism or vanity. It is an opportunity to rejoice in the good things God is doing in our lives, and to acknowledge the areas in our life that need improvement.

Measuring Discipleship

Science has created hundreds of instruments to measure the health of the human body. Some are exceedingly complex, like an MRI or a CT scan. Others are very simple, like a stethoscope or a reflex hammer. To determine the health of a patient, one instrument is not enough. The body is too complicated to be properly diagnosed by just one thing.

The same is true with our souls. Our spiritual health can not be effectively diagnosed by just one thing. Many Catholics use an examination of conscience to evaluate their holiness, and though that is an essential tool, it isn't enough. Christianity is not just about "sin management".

We would like to propose the Seven Characteristics of a Disciple as a diagnostic tool that can be used to help you assess your spiritual life. We are not suggesting it is the only tool you use, but we think it is an important one to help you gage how you are living your life as a disciple of Jesus Christ.

We introduced these characteristics at the beginning of the Discipleship Quad Process. Now, lets take a deeper look.

The Seven Characteristics

As seen in Scripture and in the lives of the saints, a disciple of Jesus Christ is someone who...

1. has their **IDENTITY** rooted in being a son/daughter of the Father,
2. is consistent in daily **PRAYER**,
3. actively participates in the grace of the **SACRAMENTS**,
4. lives in **OBEDIENCE** to the teachings of the Catholic Church,
5. participates in a **COMMUNITY** to grow in faith and support the growth of others,
6. frequently does acts of **SERVICE** out of love for God and neighbor, and
7. is enthusiastic about **SHARING** the Gospel and making disciples.

Like the parts of a body, all of these characteristics are related to each other, as shown in the "circle" diagram on the following page. They move from the interior to the exterior. So far in the Discipleship Quad Process, we have focused mostly on Identity. Identity is like the foundation of a house. If it is faulty, the house will never stand for long. That is why we have, and will continue to, focus on this characteristic.

Flowing from our Identity are the characteristics of Prayer, Sacraments, and Obedience. Notice how on the chart they straddle the line between the interior and the exterior. They are primarily interior characteristics with exterior features to them. As we have already examined, the interior life of prayer requires time and space. To grow in the interior grace of the Sacraments, one must physically go to Church (an exterior action).

The final three are primarily exterior characteristics with internal features to them: Community, Service, and Sharing. They require physical actions (exterior) but they are motivated by our interior characteristics. We will examine all of these more thoroughly in upcoming weeks.

SPIRITUAL CHECK-UP

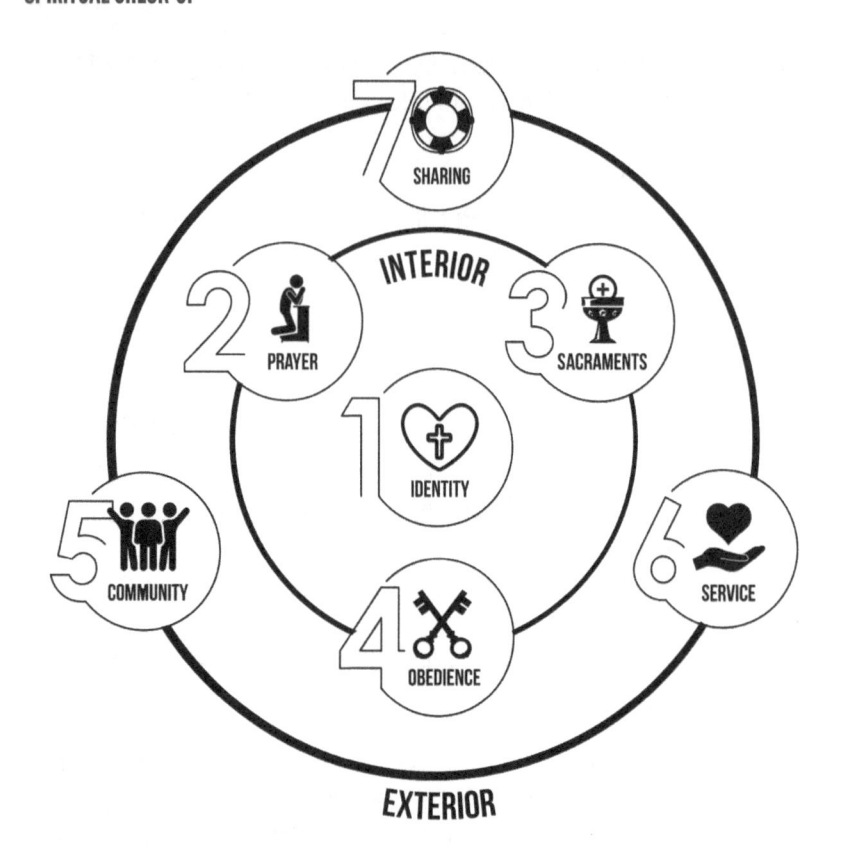

INTERIOR

1. IDENTITY
2. PRAYER
3. SACRAMENTS
4. OBEDIENCE
5. COMMUNITY
6. SERVICE
7. SHARING

EXTERIOR

Being Not Doing

The goal in assessing these characteristics is not to encourage hollow behaviors. We do not "earn" our salvation through what we do. Instead, reflecting upon our actions is like taking our temperature. If they aren't in right order, there is something off on the inside.

Thankfully, the Lord is patient with us! As St. Paul wrote to the Corinthians, "we pray for your improvement." That is what this is about. We can only grow by cooperating with the Holy Spirit.

1. What struck you from the reading?

2. Which of these characteristics do you feel you are strongest? Which characteristic do you feel like you need to grow in the most?

SPIRITUAL CHECK-UP

SCRIPTURE

The word "philosophy" is literally translated as the "love of wisdom" and there are seven books in the Old Testament dedicated to its study: Job, Psalms, Proverbs, Ecclesiastes, the Song of Songs, the Wisdom of Solomon, and Sirach (Ecclesiasticus). Unlike modern philosophies, the Scriptures emphasize that the source of all wisdom is God, and those who are truly wise are those who are obedient to him. Read **Wisdom 1:1-15.**

3. What inspired you from reading God's Word?

4. What insights did you receive from this Scripture about the importance of self-knowledge?

faith INTO life

I invite you now to prayerfully reflect upon each of the Seven Characteristics of a Disciple and circle the number (one through seven) that best represents how present it is in your life right now. There are two things to keep in mind as you do this.

First, this not an exact measurement! It is just a general sense of where you feel you are in regards to living out each characteristic. Don't spend a lot of time debating between one number or another. Your first instinct is probably the right one.

Second, your goal is to eventually get a seven for each characteristic. Giving yourself the highest mark does not mean that you are perfect! (Remember, this isn't an examination of conscience where you are reflecting on your sinfulness.) It means the Holy Spirit is working in your life so you can live as a disciple of Jesus Christ. You will notice on the scale from one to seven that the end of the line fades away. That is because there is always room to grow.

Challenge Recap

The goal of the weekly challenges has been to give you a tangible way to grow in the characteristics of Identity and Prayer. Future challenges will help you grow in other characteristics. Here is what you have been challenged to do so far:

Identity:

- Recognize an obstacle in your relationship with God, and do one thing to remove (or minimize) it.
- Identify an area in your life that needs to be "made new," and find a way to surrender that to God.
- Recognize your God-given purpose and the specific gifts he has given you to live that out.
- Surrender something that you put your trust in (over God).

SPIRITUAL CHECK-UP

- Read the Gospel of Luke.
- Memorize ("hide in your heart") 1 John 3:1.
- Do something to celebrate your baptism.

Prayer:

- Do something that will remind you of God's constant presence.
- Spend slightly more time in daily prayer (or start praying daily), and/or enhance your personal prayer space (or create one).

Your challenge for this section will ask what you might do so as to grow in the characteristics of Identity and Prayer. If you aren't sure what to do, look back at the previous challenges in that area. Perhaps there was a challenge you could have done better (do you still remember 1 John 3:1?). Perhaps there is a challenge you could do again (can you slightly add to your daily prayer time?). Or maybe there is type of challenge that you could do something similar with (you read the Gospel of Luke, what about the Gospel of Mark?).

IDENTITY: *Our identity is rooted in being a child of the Father, redeemed by the Son, and alive in the Holy Spirit. We are loved because of who we are, not what we do.*

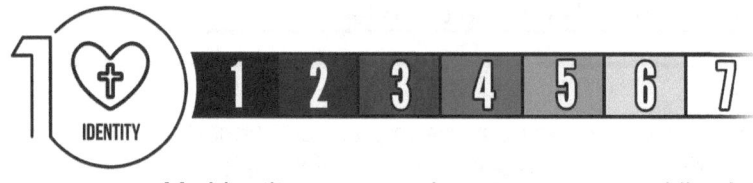

IDENTITY	1	2	3	4	5	6	7
	My identity is based on things of this world: success, appearance, possessions, etc.		I am torn between finding my identity/ self worth between God and the world.			I live in the awareness of being a child of God who is in, but not of, this world.	

5. What is one thing you can do this week to strengthen your identity as a son or daughter of God?

_____
_____
_____
_____
_____

PRAYER: *We have an active, daily life of prayer, both individually and communally, where we glorify God and seek His will. It becomes the air we breathe.*

2 PRAYER | 1 | 2 | 3 | 4 | 5 | 6 | 7 |

| I don't find time to pray. | I pray occasionally, depending on how busy the day gets. | I pray consistently, making time for personal prayer. |

6. What is one thing you can do this week to strengthen your prayer life?

_____
_____
_____
_____
_____

Establishing a Baseline

In the upcoming weeks we will explore the other characteristics. However, it is good to establish a "baseline" of where you feel you are with them right now. That way, you can see how you grow in these areas as the Discipleship Quad Process continues.

Also, at your Quad Gathering this week, you will have a chance to reflect on the commitment you signed at the beginning of the process (it can be found on the following pages).

SACRAMENTS: *We prayerfully encounter Jesus on a regular basis through the sacraments of the Church and live in the power of the grace we have received through them.*

1 2 3 4 5 6 7

| 1 — I don't receive the sacraments. | 4 — I do the basics: Mass on Sunday, Reconciliation occasionally. | 7 — I frequently receive and call upon sacramental grace. |

OBEDIENCE: *We seek to understand and obey the teachings of Christ as passed on to us through the Apostles and now living in the Magisterium of the Catholic Church.*

1 2 3 4 5 6 7

| 1 — I don't trust the teachings of the Church. | 4 — I agree with the Church on some things, other things I don't. | 7 — I believe the Holy Spirit speaks through the Church and I try to understand what she teaches. |

WEEK 13

COMMUNITY: *We participate in our parish/faith community and foster deeper relationships with individuals with whom we can share and grow in our faith.*

5 COMMUNITY

1	2	3	4	5	6	7

My faith is about "me and Jesus," I don't really need others.	I am occasionally at events where other Christians are present.	I intentionally participate in community events and try to build Christian friendships.

SERVICE: *We devote our time, talent, and treasure to our parish, our community, and to those in need, encountering Jesus in "the least of these."*

6 SERVICE

1	2	3	4	5	6	7

I'm too busy with my own things to help others.	I help those whom I love, such as my family and friends.	I seek to serve, not just family and friends, but strangers in need.

SHARING: *In both words and action, we share the Good News of Jesus Christ, and we commit ourselves to helping others be His disciples.*

7 SHARING

1	2	3	4	5	6	7

My faith is a private matter and I don't want to "push" it on others.	I think I share my faith through my actions, but don't say much about it.	In both words and actions, I am excited to share my faith and help others be disciples.

FOR YOUR ✠ GATHERING

RECALL (20-30 minutes): Begin with the Scripture and the prayer from the Front Page of the week. Then the Quad shares with each other how their week was, with a particular emphasis on how they experienced God working in their life. How did everyone do on the "This Week I Will" challenge?

REFLECT (20-30 minutes): The Quad shares how he or she answered the **FIRST FOUR** questions from the lesson, as well as any inspirations he or she received from "The Daily Bread" or their daily meditation on the main verse for the week.

RESOLVE (40-55 minutes): The facilitator says, ""In his second letter to the Corinthians, St. Paul shared about a time he was struggling, and the Lord said to him, 'My grace is sufficient for you, for my power is made perfect in weakness' (2 Corinthians 12:9). It can be overwhelming to identify areas of growth in our lives and hard to figure out where to start working on them. No matter how long we have been disciples of Jesus, there are always going to be areas where we can grow." **The Quad shares and discusses their answers to Q5 and Q6, and writes them down in the "This Week I Will" in the next week.**

Then the facilitator says, "There is one more thing we would like to evaluate this week: our Discipleship Quad Commitment that we signed together a few months ago. Let's take a moment to quietly reread it, and then share how we are doing with each of the points." After about a minute, start going through each of the five points, making them a "have I" question instead of a statement. For example: "Have I completed all assignments..." "Have I offered myself fully to the Lord..." This isn't a moment to critique each other. Instead, it is an opportunity to reflect how we might be a better support to the Quad and get more out of the experience ourselves.

DISCIPLESHIP Quad COMMITMENT

For the Quad to be a life-changing experience for yourself and others, it is important that everyone is committed to the Quad to the best of their ability.

In order to grow toward maturity in Christ and be empowered to be a disciple and disciple-maker, I commit myself to the following:

1. Complete all assignments/readings on a weekly basis, prior to my Discipleship Quad, in order to fully contribute.

2. Meet weekly with my fellow Discipleship Quad members for approximately one and one-half hours to share life and dialogue over the content of the assignments.

3. Offer myself fully to the Lord with the anticipation that I am entering a time of accelerated transformation during this discipleship period.

4. Contribute to a climate of honesty, trust, and personal vulnerability in a spirit of mutual up-building.

5. Give serious consideration to continuing the discipling chain by committing myself to invest in three other people and participate in another Discipleship Quad following the completion of this one.

In closing, ask the group what their prayer intentions are and have everyone write those down on the first page of the following week. The facilitator then introduces the topic for the next week. Then he or she says, "Let us take a moment to listen to the living Word of God," and reads the accompanying Scripture, followed by a moment of silent reflection. The session closes with the Quad saying the prayer for the next week together, followed by an Our Father and a Hail Mary.

THIS WEEK I WILL

✝ PRAYER REQUESTS

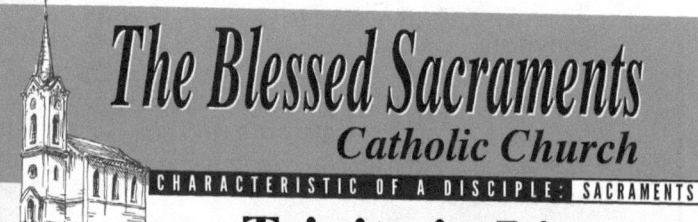

WEEK 14

The Blessed Sacraments
Catholic Church

CHARACTERISTIC OF A DISCIPLE: **SACRAMENTS**

Trinity in Liturgy

The Mass is a prayer to the Father from the Son that we participate in through the power of the Holy Spirit.

PASTOR
Fr. Francis

RETIRED PRIEST
Fr. Benedict

DEACON
Dcn. Laurence

BUSINESS MANAGER
Peter Faber

YOUTH MINISTRY
John Bosco

MUSIC MINISTRY
Cecelia Noheadia

SOUP KITCHEN
Teresa Kolkata

"For as often as you eat this bread and drink this cup, you proclaim the death of the Lord until he comes."
– *1 Corinthians 11:26*

3 SACRAMENTS

I bind unto myself the Name, the strong Name of the Trinity; by invocation of the same. The Three in One, and One in Three, of Whom all nature hath creation, Eternal Father, Spirit, Word: Praise to the Lord of my salvation, Salvation is of Christ the Lord. Amen. (St. Patrick's Breastplate)

WEEK 14

THE *Daily* BREAD

The Lord's Supper: **Matthew 26:26-30**

Jesus, the Great High Priest: **Hebrews 4:14-16**

A vision of heavenly worship: **Revelation 4:1-11**

"We should not stay away from our assembly": **Hebrews 10:19-25**

"Do this in remembrance of me": **1 Corinthians 11:23-26**

Main Verse for the Week: **1 Corinthians 11:26**

1 2 3 4 5 6 7

FAITH SEEKING UNDERSTANDING

Many who go to Mass get caught up in some of the external things: the look of the church, the music that is being played, or how good (or bad) the homily was. However, there is a much deeper reality at work.

At Mass, we participate in the perfect prayer of Jesus to the Father through the power of the Holy Spirit. We enter into the very life of the Trinity!

What Is the Trinity?

Jesus revealed to us the mystery of God's life, the Trinity: Father, Son, and Holy Spirit. God is three divine "Persons" with one divine "nature." These terms, as used by the Church (and philosophers) have different meanings than they do in everyday language.

Each of us has a "person" and a "nature." "Nature" refers to *what* I am. Like you, I have a human nature. If I had bird nature, I would fly in the air; if I had fish nature, I would live underwater. If you asked me, "What are you?", the answer would be, "human." Though you and I both have human natures, we don't have the *same* human nature. We are distinct from each other.

There is more to me than my nature. There is something unrepeatable about me that makes me unlike anything else in creation, even if someone else's nature looked exactly like mine. That essence of *who* I am is what is meant by the word "person." So, I am one human person with one human nature. You are, too.

God is three divine Persons with one divine nature. Because the Father, Son, and Holy Spirit all share the same divine ("God") nature, there is only one God. They are not each a third of God, nor do they take turns being God. The Father is God. Jesus is God. The Holy Spirit is God. If we asked him, "What are you?", he would reply, "I am God." If we asked, "Who are you?" he would reply, "I am Father, I am Son, I am Holy Spirit."

We should not be surprised that God is more complex than we are! After all, we are made in *his* image, and an image is always less than the original.

Celebrating the Father, Son, and Holy Spirit

It is important to understand the life of the Trinity because the Mass is a prayer to the Father from the Son that we participate in through the Holy Spirit.

To the Father: Everything in the liturgy is directed to the Father, the one who "so loved the world that he sent his only Son" (John 3:16). In the Mass, we adore the Father as the "source of all the blessings" (*Catechism*, 1110), which he has given us through Jesus and the Spirit.

From the Son: Jesus is the one who offers the perfect sacrifice, the perfect prayer. We enter into the moment of our salvation when Jesus died and rose again! "In the earthly liturgy we share in a foretaste of that heavenly liturgy" (*Catechism,* 1088).

Through the Holy Spirit: As we read earlier, "We do not know how to pray as we ought" … This is where the Holy Spirit comes in. The Spirit makes Christ present in our hearts and in the gathered assembly so we can enter into his prayer to the Father.

This is why we begin and end the Mass, "In the name of the Father, and the Son, and the Holy Spirit." It is all about participating in the life of the Trinity.

A Taste of Heaven

We see in the life of the Trinity a communion of Persons who share the same nature. The best way to describe this life—love, for "God is love" (1 John 4:12). Everything that the most holy Trinity has done for us, from our creation to our salvation, is so that we could live eternally in this love. This is what heaven is about.

The last book of the Bible, Revelation, is about heaven. It describes candles, incense, and worship. Readings are given from Scripture.

TRINITY IN LITURGY

There are cries of "Alleluia!", "Holy, Holy, Holy!", and "Glory to God in the highest!" There is an altar, bread, chalices, and the "Lamb of God who takes away the sins of the world."

Does that sound familiar? The liturgy is where heaven meets earth, a "foretaste of the heavenly liturgy" (*Catechism,* 1090). Scott Hahn, in *The Lamb's Supper,* wrote, "When we begin to see that heaven awaits us in the Mass, we begin already to bring our home to heaven. And we begin already to bring heaven home with us."

Be It Ever So Humble...

And yet sometimes we don't like the music. The homily goes on too long. The pew is uncomfortable. There is a kid crying behind us (or your kid is crying next to you). It doesn't seem that "heavenly."

If this is your experience (or perhaps I should say *when* this is your experience), ask for the grace to see beyond the "natural" into the "supernatural." If you had been in Bethlehem some 2,000 years ago, you likely would have missed the beauty of the Incarnation amid the stench of the animals in the manger. God likes to take natural, imperfect, and humble things and transform them into his glory.

The Front Page for Sacraments gets its look from a parish bulletin. Most of us look at the bulletin to see when sacraments are available, and the parish is the place where most sacraments are celebrated.

WEEK 14

1. What struck you from this reading?

2. How has this understanding of who God is (Trinity) help you better understand how to best worship him (Liturgy)?

TRINITY IN LITURGY

SCRIPTURE

The followers of Jesus had discovered the empty tomb and angels declared that he had risen, but no one had seen him yet. Two of the disciples left Jerusalem heading toward a town called Emmaus, when suddenly there was a stranger in their midst… **Luke 24:13-35.**

3. What inspired you from reading God's Word?

\
\
\
\
\
\
\

4. Why do you think Jesus waited to reveal himself?

faith INTO life

In our reading, Jesus walked among his disciples, though they did not recognize who he was. It says that he explained the Scriptures to them, and then they recognized him in the "breaking of the bread" (Luke 24:35). These two movements, the Word and the Eucharist, is the structure of the Mass we celebrate.

The Word and the Eucharist

As we go through the Mass, we participate in the different parts of Christ's life. We begin Mass with a Gloria (except in Advent and Lent), which is the song the angels sung when Christ was born. We then hear from the written Word of God, with the high point being the gospels (which is why we stand). That first part of the Mass is known as the Liturgy of the Word and happens primarily at the ambo, which is where the Scriptures are read.

From there we go into the second part of the Mass, the Liturgy of the Eucharist. We move from the ambo to the altar. We pray, "Hosanna in the highest!" which echoes the acclamations Jesus was given as he entered into Jerusalem on Palm Sunday. Then we sit at the table of the Last Supper, when he told his apostles to "do this in remembrance of me" (1 Corinthians 11:24). Next week, we will focus more on the sacrament of the Eucharist.

The Paschal Mystery

The suffering, death, resurrection, and ascension of Jesus are known as the "Paschal Mystery" (*pasch* means "lamb" in Latin—the Lamb of God). This is how God saved us: the Father sent the Son, the Son died and rose for us, and the Spirit now dwells in us and brings us to the Father through Jesus.

The *Catechism* says that the Mass "not only recalls the events that saved us, but actualizes them, makes them present. The Paschal Mystery of Christ is celebrated, not repeated" (1104). Let's repeat that last phrase: "The Paschal Mystery of Christ is celebrated, not repeated." Through the power of the Holy Spirit, we are brought back to the moment of our salvation: the Last Supper, the foot of the cross, the empty tomb.

That's right. *Time travel.* The Paschal Mystery stands in the center of human history. Everything led up to it; everything flows from it. We might go to Mass every day, but there is only one Paschal Mystery in which we participate. The Eucharist we receive is the same Eucharist that our pope received today, St. Therese of Lisieux received a hundred years ago, St. Francis of Assisi received 800 years ago, and the apostles received 2,000 years ago.

This is how Jesus wants us to participate in his saving work. As he said in the gospel of John, "Unless you eat of the Son of Man and drink his blood, you do not have life within you" (John 6:53—we will examine that passage next week). We can enter into the life of the Trinity through the Paschal Mystery which we celebrate at Mass.

Sent to Transform the World

The word "mass" comes from the final blessing in Latin: *Ite, missa est*, which literally means, "Go, it has been sent." What is sent? We are. Filled with Christ and the power of the Holy Spirit, we are sent to share the Father's love with the world.

Pope Benedict XVI talked about the connection with *missa* and mission:

> In antiquity, *missa* simply meant 'dismissal.' However in Christian usage it gradually took on a deeper meaning. The word 'dismissal' has come to imply a 'mission.' These few words succinctly express the missionary nature of the Church" (*Sacramentum Caritatis*, 51).

The Mass is not meant to be a personal experience that we keep to ourselves. We become living tabernacles sent forth to bring Christ to the world. The very word we use to describe what we celebrate, Mass, implies the mission of sharing Jesus to others with our words and actions. "For as often as you eat this bread and drink this cup, you proclaim the death of the Lord until he comes" (1 Corinthians 11:26). The real fruit of a well-celebrated liturgy isn't only what happens within that hour in the Church, but what the people do during the following 167 hours in the world.

Different Expressions, Same Mass

The style of the celebrations may differ, but is it always the same Mass. The musicians might play guitars and sing in Spanish, play piano and sing in English, or play the organ and sing in Latin. One liturgy might be in a Gothic cathedral, another in a small country church, and another may be hidden in a basement for fear of persecution. The words might be in Vietnamese, Latin, English, Spanish, or a mix of all of them. The homily might be short or long. There may or may not be doughnuts afterward. But it is always the same Mass, the same mission, the same mystery that we celebrate together as the people of God.

TRINITY IN LITURGY

5. What stood out to you in the reading?

6. What role does the Mass have in your relationship with God?

FOR YOUR ✝ GATHERING

RECALL (20-30 minutes): Begin with the Scripture and the prayer from the Front Page of the week. Then the Quad shares with each other how their week was, with a particular emphasis on how they experienced God working in their life. How did everyone do on the "This Week I Will" challenge?

REFLECT (50-60 minutes): The Quad shares how he or she answered the six questions from the lesson, as well as any inspirations he or she received from "The Daily Bread" or their daily meditation on the main verse for the week.

RESOLVE (10-15 minutes): The facilitator says, "The Liturgy isn't about 'what' we do as much as 'who' we worship. It is an encounter with Divine Love and a participation in the greatest act of love and mercy that ever happened! It is important that we don't just 'go through the motions' but actively participate in the celebration of the Mass. One of the best ways to do that is to not just 'show up' but prepare our hearts and minds for what we are about to do. **What is one thing you can do to better prepare yourself for worshiping the Triune God in the Mass this week?**"

Allow for a moment of silence and then discuss. Write down those resolutions on the "This Week I Will" part of the Front Page of the following week. Then the Quad shares what else they would like prayer for and writes those intentions down in the space provided.

The facilitator then introduces the topic for the next week. Then he or she says, "Let us take a moment to listen to the living Word of God," and reads the accompanying Scripture, followed by a moment of silent reflection. The session closes with the Quad saying the prayer for the next week together, followed by an Our Father and a Hail Mary.

Next week has a bonus section, Discipleship in Action!

THIS WEEK I WILL

✝ PRAYER REQUESTS

WEEK 15

The Blessed Sacraments
Catholic Church

CHARACTERISTIC OF A DISCIPLE: **SACRAMENTS**

The Bread of Life

Jesus Christ is fully present—body, blood, soul, and divinity—in the Eucharist.

PASTOR
Fr. Francis

RETIRED PRIEST
Fr. Benedict

DEACON
Dcn. Laurence

BUSINESS MANAGER
Peter Faber

YOUTH MINISTRY
John Bosco

MUSIC MINISTRY
Cecelia Noheadia

SOUP KITCHEN
Teresa Kolkata

"Whoever eats my flesh and drinks my blood has eternal life, and I will raise him up on the last day."
– John 6:54

3 SACRAMENTS

May the heart of Jesus, in the Most Blessed Sacrament, be praised, adored, and loved with grateful affection, at every moment, in all the tabernacles of the world, even to the end of time. Amen.

THE *Daily* BREAD

Multiplication of loaves: **John 6:1-15**

Changing water into wine: **John 2:1-12**

Manna from heaven: **Exodus 16:1-5**

The Last Supper: **Matthew 26:26-30**

Not just another meal: **1 Corinthians 11:27-32**

Main Verse for the Week: **John 6:54**

FAITH SEEKING UNDERSTANDING

Love is a supernatural gift. You can't quantify it like a gallon of water or a pound of gold. A larger person doesn't have a greater capacity to love than a smaller person. It can neither be measured nor bound by the physical realm.

Yet to experience love there has to be something physical to manifest it: a gift, a touch… even the sound of the words, "I love you," have a physical element to them. There is a reason why many weddings end with, "You may now kiss the bride." As physical beings, we need something tangible to express the intangible. We need something natural to express the supernatural. This is why long-distance relationships can be so difficult.

Hearing, Seeing, and Touching Love

The Father, Son, and Holy Spirit love us. God is love and has been since before there was time. Our sin did not stop God from loving us (for he can't stop being himself), but it did tarnish our experience of his love. A child who runs away from loving parents will no longer feel their love, even though that love is still there. Like the prodigal son, we ran away. The second Person of the Trinity took on our flesh to bring us back.

In that Incarnation, God took what was natural (humanity) and made it supernatural (divinity). Jesus was fully man *and* fully God. Perhaps it is our human arrogance that doesn't make us marvel at this even more than we do. How could the God of the universe confine himself in a baby at his mother's breast?

God became flesh so we could experience him, so apostles like St. John would not talk about God as a concept but as "what we have heard, what we have seen with our eyes, what we looked upon and touched with our hands" (1 John 1:1). This wasn't just his plan for those who were alive 2,000 years ago and the rest of us missed out. God's desire is that we would still be able to see, hear, and feel him. This is what he does through the sacraments.

A Kiss from God

The *Catechism* describes sacraments as "efficacious signs of grace, instituted by Christ and given to the Church, by which the divine life is dispensed to us" (1131). An "efficacious sign" is something symbolic that brings about something real. A kiss between husband and wife can be considered an "efficacious sign," as it physically communicates the love between them and makes it real. In a similar way, every sacrament can be seen as a kiss from God!

The sacraments can also be seen as CPR, for God does more than kiss us—he breathes his divine life into our lungs. This is how God gives his life to us. The sacraments are not just *a* way to experience God, they are *the* way. Jesus instituted them and is at work in them through the Holy Spirit: "As fire transforms into itself everything it touches, so the Holy Spirit transforms into the divine life whatever is subjected to its power" (*Catechism*, 1127).

Signs into Reality

The signs of what would become sacraments had been a part of Judaism from the beginning. For example, the Jews were baptizing people before Jesus came (Jesus himself was baptized by John the Baptist). But that wasn't a sacrament; it was just symbolic.

In the Paschal Mystery, Jesus transformed those signs to become "efficacious." They now *make happen* what they signify! St. Peter wrote, "[The flood at the time of Noah] prefigured baptism, which saves you now. It is not a removal of dirt from the body but an appeal to God for a clear conscience, through the resurrection of Jesus Christ" (1 Peter 3:19-22). He is letting Christians know that though they might have been familiar with baptism before, through Jesus it is something *new*. It isn't just "a removal of dirt from the body" but a sacrament "which saves you now."

An Intimate Encounter with Jesus

When you were baptized, it was Jesus who baptized you. When the bishop laid his hands on you in the sacrament of Confirmation, it was Jesus who touched you. When you heard the words in Reconciliation, "I absolve you of all your sins," it was Jesus who said that. And in the Eucharist, the "sacrament of sacraments," we receive Jesus himself: body, blood, soul, and divinity.

God does not want a long-distance relationship with us. He is truly present in the sacraments. It is the most intimate way to be with him in this life and gives us the grace we need to be with him forever in the next.

1. What struck you from this reading?

2. Has your experience of sacraments felt more like a ritual or an encounter with Jesus, a person who loves you?

THE BREAD OF LIFE

SCRIPTURE

Jesus had just fed 5,000 men (not including women and children) and then walked on the water to escape the crowds (John 6:1-21). When they caught up to him, they wanted more food. Jesus wanted to give them something more than that and taught them something that was so difficult for them to understand that many disciples left him because of it. Read **John 6:22-69.**

3. What inspired you from reading God's Word?

4. "Do not work for food that perishes but for the food that endures for eternal life" (John 6:27). How does that apply to your life?

faith INTO life

Eucharist means "thanksgiving." The Jews used that word to respond to what God had done in their lives. As followers of Christ, the thing we are most thankful for is Jesus' death and resurrection (the Paschal Mystery), which is what the Eucharist is all about. As can be seen in Scripture, God had prepared the Church for the gift of the Eucharist from the very beginning.

Gifts of Bread and Wine

The first appearance of bread and wine is found in the book of Genesis. It was brought to Abraham, our father in faith, by a mysterious figure named Melchizedek, a "priest of God Most High" (Genesis 14:18). Our Catholic faith sees this as a foreshadowing of the Eucharist that will be given to us through our priests.

When God was about to liberate his people from the Egyptians, he had them celebrate what would become their highest holy feast, Passover. It involved unleavened bread (so they could eat it on the journey, since leavened bread would grow stale) and wine (to celebrate their freedom). It was the Passover feast where Jesus celebrated his Last Supper and instituted the Eucharist.

What Is That?

As the Israelites wandered in the wilderness, they grew hungry and were on the verge of starvation. So, God sent down bread from heaven. They didn't know what kind of bread it was, so they called it *manna*, which is Hebrew for, "What is that?"

Just as the Jews in the Old Testament did not know what the "bread from heaven" was, many Jews in the New Testament did not understand the "Living Bread" who stood right in front of them. When Jesus said, "I am the living bread," they were confused. When he said, "you have to eat my flesh and drink my blood," they thought he was crazy.

THE BREAD OF LIFE

More Than a Parable

Our Protestant brothers and sisters suggest that John 6 is a parable of Jesus, not meant to be taken literally. If this was so, then why did he allow so many disciples to leave him without explaining what he meant?

Usually when Jesus taught a parable, he would then explain it to his apostles. But not here. Instead, he turned to them and said, "Do you want to go, too?" He meant what he said. Though St. Peter did not understand what he meant (at the time), he had faith to trust that what he said was true.

The Eucharist and the cross are stumbling blocks. It is the same mystery, and it never ceases to be an occasion of division. "Will you also go away?": the Lord's question echoes through the ages, as a loving invitation to discover that only he has "the words of eternal life" and that to receive in faith the gift of his Eucharist is to receive the Lord himself (*Catechism,* 1336).

I had a similar experience in my own life. Like the Jews at the time of Christ, the first time I heard that the Eucharist was the Body and Blood of Jesus, I was incredulous. But then I had an insight similar to one that St. Ambrose had: "Could not Christ's word, which can make from nothing what did not exist, change existing things into what they were not before?" If God could create the universe with a command, how hard would it be for him to change bread and wine into his Body and Blood?

Source and Summit

The Eucharist is the "source and summit" of our Catholic faith (*Catechism* 1324). It is called the "sacrament of sacraments" because all the other sacraments culminate in it. St. Irenaeus wrote, "Our way of thinking is attuned to the Eucharist," meaning that everything we do in our faith has Christ in the Eucharist at its center. Celebrating the Eucharist isn't just *a* thing we do as Catholics, it is *the* thing!

The blessings we receive from the Eucharist are too numerous to mention. It strengthens our union with Christ, separates us from sin, gives strength to grow in virtue, unites us together as a community of faith, helps us see Jesus in the poor (for if we can recognize him in what was bread and wine, how much more will we see him in the faces of those in need?), and it anticipates our eternal glory.

The Real Presence

The Eucharist is known as the "Real Presence." Jesus is present to us in many ways in the Church:

> ... in his word, in his Church's prayer, 'where two or three are gathered in my name,' in the poor, the sick, and the imprisoned, in the sacraments of which he is the author, in the sacrifice of the Mass, and in the person of the minister. But he is present... most especially in the Eucharistic species (*Catechism,* 1373).

His presence in the Eucharist is "veiled." We still only see and taste what was bread and wine, just as those who met Christ 2,000 years ago saw what appeared to be a normal person.

The Body of Christ that we receive in the Eucharist is not a piece of a dead body. It is the wholeness of Jesus' living body. He gives himself to us *entirely* in the Eucharist. What can we say in response to such a gift? "Lord, I am not worthy to receive you."

How much more can he love us?

THE BREAD OF LIFE

5. What stood out to you in the reading?

6. How has this lesson helped you to see the Eucharist in a new way?

The next page has a bonus section, Discipleship in Action!

DISCIPLESHIP IN ACTION

Spending an hour before the Eucharist, either exposed in Adoration or reposed in the tabernacle, is a practice that the Church has been encouraging for centuries. It is hard to find a saint who did not write about how important it was in his or her life.

Bl. Fulton Sheen was a bishop in the Archdiocese of New York and was a popular radio and television personality. He encouraged Catholics to try to spend an hour every day before the Blessed Sacrament. Depending on your current state of life, this might not be something you are ready to jump right into, especially if the practice is new to you. However, we'd like to encourage you to try to do a holy hour once a week.

Since Bl. Fulton Sheen was such a good communicator, I'll let him explain about it himself. The following are excerpts from his autobiography, *Treasure in Clay*, from the twelfth chapter titled, "The Hour that Makes My Day":

> First, the holy hour is not a devotion; it is a sharing in the work of redemption. Our Blessed Lord used the words 'hour' and 'day' in two totally different connotations in the gospel of John. "Day" belongs to God; the 'hour' belongs to evil. Seven times in the gospel of John, the word 'hour' is used, and in each instance it refers to the demonic, and to the moments when Christ is no longer in the Father's hands, but in the hands of men. In the garden, Our Lord contrasted two 'hours'—one was the evil hour; 'this is your hour'—with which Judas could turn out the lights of the world. In contrast, Our Lord asked: 'Could you not watch one hour with me?' In other words, he asked for an hour of reparation to combat the hour of evil; an hour of victimal union with the cross to overcome the anti-love of sin.

Secondly, the only time Our Lord asked the apostles for anything was the night he went into his agony. Then he did not ask all of them... perhaps because he knew he could not count on their fidelity. But at least he expected three to be faithful to him: Peter, James and John. As often in the history of the Church since that time, evil was awake, but the disciples were asleep. That is why there came out of his anguished and lonely heart the sigh: 'Could you not watch one hour with me?' Not for an hour of activity did he plead, but for an hour of companionship.

The third reason I keep up the holy hour is to grow more and more into his likeness. As Paul puts it: 'We are transfigured into his likeness, from splendor to splendor.' We become like that which we gaze upon. Looking into a sunset, the face takes on a golden glow. Looking at the Eucharistic Lord for an hour transforms the heart in a mysterious way as the face of Moses was transformed after his companionship with God on the mountain. Something happens to us similar to that which happened to the disciples at Emmaus. On Easter Sunday afternoon when the Lord met them, he asked why they were so gloomy. After spending some time in his presence, and hearing again the secret of spirituality—'The Son of Man must suffer to enter into his glory'—their time with him ended, and their 'hearts were on fire.'

I have found that it takes some time to catch fire in prayer. This has been one of the advantages of the daily hour. It is not so brief as to prevent the soul from collecting itself and shaking off the multitudinous distractions of the world. Sitting before the Presence is like a body exposing itself before the sun to absorb its rays. Silence in the hour is a tête-à-tête with the Lord. In those moments, one does not so much pour out written prayers, but listening takes its place. We do not say: 'Listen, Lord, for thy servant speaks,' but 'Speak, Lord, for thy servant heareth.'

So the holy hour, quite apart from all its positive spiritual benefits, kept my feet from wandering too far. Being tethered to a tabernacle, one's rope for finding other pastures is not so long. That dim tabernacle lamp, however pale and faint, had some mysterious luminosity to darken the brightness of 'bright lights.' The holy hour became like an oxygen tank to revive the breath of the Holy Spirit in the midst of the foul and fetid atmosphere of the world. Even when it seemed so unprofitable and lacking in spiritual intimacy, I still had the sensation of being at least like a dog at the master's door, ready in case he called me.

I'll close with one more quote from Bl. Sheen: "A Holy Hour of Adoration in our modern rat race is necessary for authentic prayer." As he did with Sts. Peter, James, and John in the garden, Jesus is inviting you to spend an hour with him in the Eucharist.

FOR YOUR ✝ GATHERING

RECALL (20-30 minutes): Begin with the Scripture and the prayer from the Front Page of the week. Then the Quad shares with each other how their week was, with a particular emphasis on how they experienced God working in their life. How did everyone do on the "This Week I Will" challenge?

REFLECT (50-60 minutes): The Quad shares how he or she answered the six questions from the lesson, as well as any inspirations he or she received from "The Daily Bread" or their daily meditation on the main verse for the week.

RESOLVE (10-15 minutes): The facilitator says, "God does not want a 'long distance' relationship with us. He went to great lengths to become physically close to us in all of the sacraments, and especially the Eucharist. Jesus became flesh, suffered, died, and rose from the dead so he could be near us in the Eucharist. We should try to be near him as well, not just spiritually but also physically. **This week, can you make a commitment to visit Jesus in the Eucharist for fifteen, thirty, or sixty minutes?**"

Discuss. This can be done by staying early or late before the Sunday Mass. It would be even better if there were an adoration chapel that could be visited during the week. If it can't happen this week, could it happen the following week? Might any of the Quad be able to do it together? Write down those resolutions on the "This Week I Will" part of the Front Page of the following week. Then the Quad shares what else they would like prayer for and writes those intentions down in the space provided.

The facilitator then introduces the topic for the next week. Then he or she says, "Let us take a moment to listen to the living Word of God," and reads the accompanying Scripture, followed by a moment of silent reflection. The session closes with the Quad saying the prayer for the next week together, followed by an Our Father and a Hail Mary.

The next week has a bonus section, Going Deeper!

How is your daily prayer going?

If you have time in your Q Gathering, discuss how you are doing with your daily prayer. Have you been able to be faithful to it? If not, what has gotten in the way? If you have, might you be able to spend a few more minutes each day in prayer?

THIS WEEK I WILL

✝ PRAYER REQUESTS

WEEK 16

CATHOLICISM 101
The Living Word

God reveals himself to us through the Church.

> "Indeed, the word of God is living and effective, sharper than any two-edged sword, penetrating even between soul and spirit, joints and marrow, and able to discern reflections and thoughts of the heart."
> — Hebrews 4:12

CHARACTERISTIC OF A DISCIPLE: OBEDIENCE

Lord, thank you for giving us the one, holy, catholic, and apostolic church. You speak your word through her. Continue to guide and protect her as your bride, and help us to trust her as we trust you. Amen.

4 — OBEDIENCE

THE *Daily* BREAD

WEEK 16

The rock on which the Church is built: **Matthew 16:13-20**

Paul entrusting Timothy to pass on the faith: **1 Timothy 1:12-20**

Not just human teaching: **1 Thessalonians 2:1-13**

"Be faithful to what you have learned": **2 Timothy 3:10-17**

"Be subject to the presbyters": **1 Peter 5:1-11**

Main Verse for the Week: **Hebrews 4:12**

① ② ③ ④ ⑤ ⑥ ⑦

FAITH SEEKING UNDERSTANDING

How do we know what we know about God? There are plenty of religions out there, so which one is right? In our pluralistic society today, many shrug and say, "I guess they are all right, in their own way." It seems arrogant to say that one religion is true and another is false.

Many religions, movements, philosophies, and spiritualities can be described as "humanity's search for God." However, the Bible tells a different story.

It is about God's search for *us*.

An Intimate Knowledge

God *wants* us to know about him. Why? Because there is a connection between "knowing" and "loving." The more we learn about a friend, the deeper our connection. We might pass by strangers who we have a lot in common with, but it is our lack of knowledge that keeps us from a relationship.

The word that Scripture uses to describe how God shares himself with us is "revelation." In Greek, this word meant, "unveiling," and referred to the first moment of intimacy between a husband and wife. The scriptures frequently compare the love of God to a marriage. The final book of the Bible, Revelation, says that heaven is a wedding feast of the Lamb of God (Jesus) and his bride, the Church (us).

So, God doesn't want us to know facts like we might learn about a historical figure. He desires an *intimate* knowledge, the kind of knowledge that a husband would have of his bride, and vice versa.

God Takes the Initiative

St. John wrote, "In this is love: not that we have loved God, but that he loved us" (1 John 4:10). He is the one who takes the initiative in our relationship. He desired to "walk with us in the garden" as he did with Adam and Eve. And when that relationship was broken by sin, he did not abandon us.

He called Abraham to be the father of a "chosen people." He called Moses to lead those people out of slavery and into a promised land. He called Deborah to rally her people against their oppressors. He called David to make them into a kingdom. He called Mary to bear a son. With every call, every prophet, and every covenant, we learned more and more about who he was and how he loved us.

Finally, he came himself in the Person of Jesus Christ. He wants more than just to save us. He isn't like a superhero who swoops in, saves the day, then flies away until the next crisis. God—the Father, Son, and Holy Spirit—wants us to fall in love with him as he is in love with us. That means we have to be able to know him, and that is why he created the Church.

The Church

At the end of the gospel of Matthew, Jesus tells his apostles, "Go, therefore, and make disciples of all nations… teaching them everything that I have taught you" (Matthew 28:19). This is the mission statement of the Church! The Church was not an afterthought, it was his plan all along. He revealed himself to the apostles, and the apostles reveal God to us. When we profess that our Church is "one, holy, catholic, and apostolic," we are saying that we believe in what the apostles passed down to us, both orally and in writing.

So, how do we know what we know about God? We know these things through the Church which God established to share himself with us.

THE LIVING WORD

1. What struck you from this reading?

2. How do you approach learning more about the faith: as a subject to be studied or a person to love? How do you think you came to approach the faith in this way?

The next page has a bonus section, Going Deeper!

WEEK 16

Going Deeper

We occasionally add a "Going Deeper" section when we feel there is more to say than what is included in "Faith Seeking Understanding."

The Bible is so much more than a book. It is a library. It holds 73 different works, written by over 30 authors in a 1,500-year time span! What makes it so powerful is that it is not just the word of men, but the Word of God.

Divine Authorship

Though many human authors were inspired to write it, God is the author of Sacred Scripture. That is a bold statement that deserves a closer look. How can we say that? Well, first of all, this is what Scripture says of itself. St. Paul's second letter to Timothy says that Scripture is "inspired by God." Another translation says that Scripture is "God-breathed." Both Jews and Christians have held these words to be sacred, a divine communication from God.

Second, there is something different about these words. If God were to write a book, what impact would it have on human history? The Bible is the most influential book ever written and is even more popular today than it was 2,000 years ago. It is a "living" Word that changes lives. Other books come and go, but the Bible remains.

Inerrancy

Because Scripture is authored by God, we believe it to be inerrant, that is, without error. The Bible is true in everything it wants to communicate to us. At times, people have tried to disprove the Bible based on something it wasn't trying to say. The most famous example the argument that God created the world in seven days, though the Bible says that God didn't create a sun or moon until the third "day"—so how could there be a 24-hour period before that?

Like any library, there are different genres of literature. The Psalms is a book of poetry. The book of Wisdom is a book of philosophy. Isaiah is a book of prophecy. The Gospel of Matthew is an eye-witness account. The book of Genesis includes stories orally passed on for centuries among the Jewish people before being written down. (That isn't to suggest that figures such as Noah and Abraham did not exist, but that the author[s] of that book tell their stories in a more "mythological" style, which was the way stories were told in that time.) In order to understand Scripture, "the reader must take into account the conditions of their time and culture, the literary genres in use at that time, and the modes of feeling, speaking, and narrating then current" (*Catechism,* 110).

Scripture Is the "Heart of Christ"

St. Thomas Aquinas, one of the greatest theologians and philosophers of the Church, wrote that Scripture can rightfully be called the "heart of Christ" because this is where we learn about him (*Catechism,* 112). St. Jerome famously said, "Ignorance of Scripture is ignorance of Christ."

Scripture is the "speech of God as it is put down in writing under the breath of the Holy Spirit" (*Catechism,* 81). It is the most important book in human history. No other writing has had the impact the Bible has had on humanity. It shows us the way to salvation and turns sinners into saints.

Scripture should be read in the way it was intended to be read: this is God's love letter to humanity. It is at times mysterious and even confusing, as scholars debate over what some passages mean. But its overall message is clear and unified: "God so loved the world that he sent his only son, so that through him we might not perish but have eternal life" (John 3:16).

Praying with the Scriptures

The early Church adopted a practice called "divine reading" or, in Latin, *lectio divina.* It is a simple way of prayerfully reading the Bible and has five movements: Prepare, Read, Reflect, Respond, and Rest.

Prepare: Take a moment before reading the scriptures to put yourself in the presence of God. Ask the Holy Spirit to come more deeply into your heart and to open your eyes in a new way to his Word.

Read: Slowly read through the passage. At some point, a word, phrase, or sentence will jump out at you.

Reflect: Read it again, allowing yourself to be drawn into those words. Don't overthink or go into "study mode." Focus on the part that drew your attention in the first reading.

Respond: Read it a third time, and apply it to your life. Journaling can be a good exercise in this movement.

Rest: You are in the presence of God now. You've read his living Word. Take some time to rest in his love. When distractions come, turn your heart back to the Lord.

Try this with your daily readings at the end of each session, and I'm sure you will have a deeper encounter with Jesus through his Word!

The Front Page for Obedience gets its look from a student's notebook. The Church is our mother and our teacher, and we should take note of what she tells us!

THE LIVING WORD

SCRIPTURE

This is from St. John, the youngest apostle who ended up taking care of Jesus' mother, Mary, and the only apostle who was not martyred (he was under "house arrest" on the island of Patmos in modern-day Greece): **1 John 1:1-10**. (1 John is the first letter of John, which is different from the gospel of John.)

3. What inspired you from reading God's Word?

4. How does St. John say we should "live in the light"? What does that mean to you?

faith INTO life

You can hear the enthusiasm of St. John in the beginning of his first letter. He is so excited to share what he experienced! This is an important part of our faith: it is *experienced*. This isn't a new philosophy or self-help advice. The apostles, like St. John, all heard, saw, and touched the Incarnate Word, Jesus Christ. It was real. It was such a powerful experience, they couldn't help but share it with everyone they met, even if it meant that the majority of them were killed for it.

In the gospel of Matthew, Jesus told St. Peter, "You are Peter, and upon this rock I will build my Church... I will give you the keys to the kingdom of heaven" (Matthew 16:18-19). This hearkened back to the kingdom that God established under King David, where the "keys" were handed down from king to king. In the same way, the apostles handed on their authority from one generation to the next. This is known as "apostolic succession."

Tradition and Scripture

St. Paul told the Church in Thessalonica, "Stand firm and hold fast to the traditions you were taught, either by an oral statement or a letter of ours" (2 Thessalonians 2:15). Some of what the apostles taught were spoken, other teachings were written down. These teachings became known as the "deposit of faith," and it was made up of tradition (which is all the apostles taught) and Scripture (that which was written down).

The early Church was persecuted and was not able to gather publicly until the fourth century when Rome was conquered by Constantine and Christianity was declared the official religion. That is when the Church's leaders were able to come together (in what became known as "ecumenical councils") to clarify teachings about Jesus. They also clarified what was the inspired written Word of God (Scripture) and what wasn't.

Scripture Alone?

It wasn't until the 16th century that the need for a teaching authority in the Church, known as the Magisterium, was questioned. Martin Luther believed that you only needed Scripture to know Jesus, and the rest of the teaching (such as the authority of the pope) was invalid. It is worth mentioning that at that time there was a lot of corruption in the life of the Church, and there were many within the Church calling for a greater holiness among her leaders. However, the teaching of the Church wasn't wrong; it was the behavior of her members (which is a constant problem!).

Luther tried to separate Scripture from tradition and thought this would bring about a truer faith. The result? Over 10,000 denominations of Christianity. It is not to say that people who only believe in Scripture don't know or love Jesus! But why did Jesus establish a Church on Peter if he wanted his people to be so divided? Scripture was not meant to stand on its own; it was always meant to be read in the context of the tradition passed down through the Magisterium.

The Word Alive in the Mass

The Catechism of the Catholic Church, which we have often quoted, is a beautiful summary of the Deposit of Faith. The majority of the footnotes are from Scripture (70 percent!), which shows how important the Bible is in our faith. For St. Paul wrote, "All Scripture is inspired by God" (2 Timothy 3:16).

At times, Catholics are accused of not believing in the Bible. This isn't true. We believe that the Bible is at the heart of our faith, but we also believe that it is meant to be read in the context of the tradition that was handed down to us from the apostles ("either by an oral statement or a letter of ours") and those they chose to succeed them, even to the present day.

Whereas some would point to the Bible as the visual expression of what they believe, as Catholics we point to the Mass. This is the celebration passed down to us for over 2,000 years, and Scripture is *everywhere* in it—not just in the readings, but in almost every prayer, as well.

The Living Word

When we refer to the "Word of God," it is not exclusively the Bible, but the entirety of the deposit of faith. There are countless men and women who gave their lives defending this "Word" that had been handed down to them (every pope was a martyr until the fourth century!). Why would they do that? Because our faith is more than a bunch of rules and religious trivia; it is "living and effective."

This Word is the life of the Church. This is how we encounter God's love.

If you want to read a great book on Church history, I recommend *A Concise History of the Catholic Church* by Alan Schreck. It gives a great "bird's eye" view of the ups and downs of the Church, with an emphasis on how the Holy Spirit has upheld and sustained it, even in its darkest times!

And if you want to know more about what we have in common and how we differ from our Protestant brothers and sisters, I recommend another book by Alan Schreck: *Catholic and Christian*. It is amazing!

THE LIVING WORD

5. What stood out to you in the reading?

6. As you've been reading the Bible and reflecting on Church teachings over the past couple of months, how have you experienced them to be "living and effective"?

FOR YOUR ✝ GATHERING

RECALL (20-30 minutes): Begin with the Scripture and the prayer from the Front Page of the week. Then the Quad shares with each other how their week was, with a particular emphasis on how they experienced God working in their life. How did everyone do on the "This Week I Will" challenge?

REFLECT (50-60 minutes): The Quad shares how he or she answered the six questions from the lesson, as well as any inspirations he or she received from "The Daily Bread" or their daily meditation on the main verse for the week.

RESOLVE (10-15 minutes): The facilitator says, "Jesus speaks his Word through the Church. The Bible isn't ancient history; the doctrines aren't just a list of rules. God's Word is not only about what he wants of us, but more importantly it is about who he is. He desires to be intimate with us. One powerful way to be intimate with him is to allow his Word to dwell in our heart. That is why memorizing Scripture is so important. We have already memorized 1 John 3:1. **This week's challenge is to memorize another verse, Lamentations 3:22-23.**"

Challenge for the Week: Memorize Lamentations 3:22-23

Next week's verse is a profound reminder of the unchanging love of God: "The Lord's acts of mercy are not exhausted, his compassion is not spent; they are renewed each morning—great is your faithfulness!" (Lamentations 3:22-23). This is a great verse for us to "hide in your heart", especially when we get frustrated with our own sinfulness. We may be tempted to think that God's mercy will eventually run out on us, or that he will get sick of loving us. Praise God he isn't like we are! Every day there is new mercy, new grace. He is faithful, even when we are not.

If you are familiar with "Seven Nation Army" by the White Stripes, the bass line works really well for this song. If you've ever been to a sporting event or heard a high school marching band, you will recognize it.

THE LIVING WORD

The Lord's ac-cts of mercy
Are no-ot exhausted
His compassion is not spent
They are renewed each morning
Great is your faithfulness!

As I mentioned last time, the action of writing something makes a stronger impression on your brain. Use the below lines to write out the verse.

_____

_____

_____

_____

_____

The most important thing is *repetition.* Frequently repeat the verse to yourself everyday. God wants you to do this, so ask the Holy Spirit to help you remember his Word!

Speaking of repetition, write out 1 John 3:1 from memory below. If you can't remember it, then you can also use this week to remind yourself of this verse.

_____

_____

_____

_____

_____

Write down your resolution to memorize Lamentations 3:22-23 (and 1 John 3:1, if you have forgotten it) on the "This Week I Will" part of the Front Page of the following week. Then the Quad shares what else they would like prayer for and writes those intentions down in the space provided.

The facilitator then introduces the topic for the next week. Then he or she says, "Let us take a moment to listen to the living Word of God," and reads the accompanying Scripture, followed by a moment of silent reflection. The session closes with the Quad saying the prayer for the next week together, followed by an Our Father and a Hail Mary.

THIS WEEK I WILL

✙ PRAYER REQUESTS

WEEK 17

The Daily Disciple

JESUS I TRUST IN YOU!

You can always, always, always trust in God's mercy.

"The Lord's acts of mercy are not exhausted, his compassion is not spent; they are renewed each morning—great is your faithfulness!"
—Lamentations 3:22-23

CHARACTERISTIC OF A DISCIPLE: IDENTITY

O Greatly Merciful God, fill us with Your grace and keep on increasing Your mercy in us, that we may faithfully do Your holy will all through our lives and at the hour of death. Amen. (Prayer of St. Faustina)

IDENTITY

THE *Daily* BREAD

WEEK 17

The call of Zacchaeus: **Luke 19:1-10**

We must acknowledge our sins: **1 John 1:5-10**

"As far as the east is from the west": **Psalm 103:1-18**

The appeal to be reconciled: **2 Corinthians 5:17-21**

The call of St. Matthew: **Matthew 9:9-13**

Main Verse for the Week: **Lamentations 3:22-23**

① ② ③ ④ ⑤ ⑥ ⑦

FAITH SEEKING UNDERSTANDING

Perhaps you have seen the image of Divine Mercy. In it, Jesus points to his heart, and rays of red and blue stream forth, symbolizing the blood and water that flowed from his pierced side on the cross. The bottom of the picture reads, "Jesus, I trust in you." That image came from a vision that was given to St. Maria Faustina Kowalska (1905-1938), a religious sister in Poland who had visions of Jesus and also heard him talking to her. She recorded those conversations in her diary. St. John Paul II canonized her in the year 2000 and proclaimed the Sunday after Easter to be "Divine Mercy Sunday," in large part based on her writings.

What was the message that Jesus gave to St. Faustina? "Proclaim that mercy is the greatest attribute of God. All the works of My hands are crowned with mercy" (*Diary of St. Maria Faustina Kowalska*, 301).

Love and Mercy

One might have thought that love would be the greatest attribute of God, not mercy. However, St. John Paul II makes it clear that they are the same thing: "Mercy is an indispensable dimension of love; it is as it were love's second name and, at the same time, the specific manner in which love is revealed" (*Dives in Misericordia*, 7).

We experience God's love through his mercy. To acknowledge his love for us includes recognizing his mercy toward us, for without that "indispensable dimension of love" we can't experience anything of his glory. The best example of this is when God became flesh and dwelt among us. What was the name he chose to be called? In Hebrew the name "Jesus" was pronounced *Yeshua*, which is translated as, "God saves." The very name God wanted to be called meant mercy.

Trusting in Mercy

In her diary, St. Faustina said that one of the things that upset Jesus the most was that people didn't trust in his mercy: "Oh how much I am hurt by a soul's distrust! Such a soul professes that I am holy and just, but does not believe that I am Mercy and does not trust in my goodness" (*Diary*, 300). This is why Jesus asked her to put the phrase, "Jesus, I trust in you!" at the bottom of the image of Divine Mercy.

I must confess that many times in my life I have doubted God's mercy. I go to Confession and confess the same sins over and over. I become sick of my sinfulness and so I assume that God must feel the same way. He doesn't. His love never ceases, his mercy never comes to an end (this week's memorized verse). His death and resurrection overcame the sin of the world—everything that had happened and will happen until the end of time. It is my pride that tricks me into thinking that there is something I could do that would be too great for his love. St. Faustina frequently compared our sin as a drop of water compared to God's ocean of mercy for us:

> O my Jesus, your goodness surpasses all understanding, and no one will exhaust your mercy. Damnation is for the soul who wants to be damned; but for the one who desires salvation, there is the inexhaustible ocean of the Lord's mercy to draw from. How can a small vessel contain the unfathomable ocean? (*Diary*, 631).

A Divine Perspective

One reason for our lack of trust is that we can think of God's love as human, not divine. It is hard for us to comprehend unconditional love. Our human weakness struggles with forgiving the same person for the same thing, over and over again. At some point we say, "Enough!" But Jesus, even after having been betrayed by his friends, whipped to near death, made to carry a cross, stripped of his clothing, and nailed to a beam of wood while people laughed at him, did not say, "Enough!" Instead, he said, "Father, forgive them, for they know not what they do" (Luke 23:34).

JESUS I TRUST IN YOU!

God is not surprised by our sin. In fact, he is outside of time, so he can see everything we have done and will do. I often reflect on that when I begin to doubt his mercy. He knew full well every sin that I would commit in my lifetime, and yet he still died for me. "God proves his love for us in this, that while we were still sinners, Christ died for us" (Romans 5:8). The real challenge of God's mercy is not if he will forgive us, but will we let ourselves be forgiven? Or will our pride get in the way? For as St. John wrote, "If we confess our sins, he is faithful and just and will forgive our sins and cleanse us from any wrongdoing" (1 John 1:9).

Jesus, I trust in you!

The Front Page for Identity gets its look from a newspaper, because a newspaper is new every morning, just as the Father's love is. Also, it is important that our commitment as a disciple is renewed every morning.

1. What struck you from this reading?

2. Do you struggle with letting God forgive you?

SCRIPTURE

The gospel of Luke included many parables of mercy, the most famous of which are found in **Luke 15**.

3. What inspired you from reading God's Word?

4. To which son do you relate more to, the "prodigal" or the dutiful one who stayed home?

faith INTO life

These beautiful parables have many layers to them, and they cannot be fully captured in a few short paragraphs. Books have been written on the parable of the prodigal son alone. I hope these reflections may give you deeper insight into what Jesus taught about the mercy of God.

Four Lost Things

This chapter tells of four things that are lost: a sheep, a coin, a prodigal son, and a dutiful one. The reasons for why they are lost are all different, as are the reasons why people don't experience God's mercy. The sheep goes astray out of ignorance—it wasn't trying to escape the shepherd's protection. There are many born within the Church who "wander" because they don't realize what they leave behind. The coin, an inanimate object, was lost at no fault of its own, as are those who have never had the chance to hear of the mercy of God.

The prodigal son is a story of willful disobedience—perhaps this is why it speaks to our heart. He knows the father, yet still wants to waste his money on sinful things. How often have we willfully walked away from God, doing what we know to be wrong? Finally, the older brother is lost because he won't go in and celebrate the father's mercy toward the younger. The parable ends on a stirring image: the father pleads with the older son to come in the house. Will he accept the invitation, or will his self-righteousness keep him outside? It is a question we should all ask of ourselves.

A God Who Searches for Us

One thing these parables have in common is how God takes the initiative to search for what is lost. The shepherd left the other sheep to find the lost one, as was his duty. The woman searched her house for the lost coin (in the time of Christ, the mark of a married woman was a headdress with ten coins on it, so it would have been the equivalent of losing a wedding ring). When the prodigal son headed home, the father saw him "while he was still a long way off," which implied he was on the lookout for him. When the dutiful son refused to come inside, the father came out to plead with him.

Jesus said, "For the Son of Man has come to seek and to save what was lost" (Luke 19:10). It is one of the most striking characteristics of Christianity, even compared to Judaism. Reflecting on these parables, William Barclay, a famous Bible scholar, wrote:

> No Pharisee had ever dreamed of a God like that. A great Jewish scholar has admitted that this is the one absolutely new thing which Jesus taught men about God--that he actually searched for men. The Jew might have agreed that if a man came crawling home to God in self-abasement and prayed for pity he might find it; but he would never have conceived of a God who went out to search for sinners (*Commentary on Luke*, ch. 15).

God's Cause for Rejoicing

If it is surprising that God would search for us, it is even more surprising to hear that he rejoices when we are found! The shepherd did not get mad at the lost sheep for going astray. The father didn't even lecture the son after he had squandered all of the money. Each of these parables of God's mercy end with a *celebration*: "In the same way, I tell you, there will be rejoicing among the angels of God over one sinner who repents" (Luke 15:10).

This is another way in which God is not like man. We often forgive each other reluctantly. We want to make sure the other has learned a lesson and that it won't happen again. We base our mercy on the emotion expressed in the apology.

That is why the reaction of the father is so baffling. Who throws a party for a son that recklessly threw his inheritance away on wild living? Who would be so excited about forgiving someone that they don't even seem to care about what they had done?

I wouldn't. You probably wouldn't. But God does: "For my thoughts are not your thoughts, nor are your ways my ways" (Isaiah 55:8). Thank God for that!

Barriers for Reconciliation

The shepherd finds the sheep. The woman finds the coin. The son is welcomed with open arms. From what we read, there are only three things that can keep us from experiencing God's merciful love:

- **Not asking for mercy:** The first is if the son didn't come home. He could have lived the rest of his life longing to eat the food that pigs ate, never "coming to his senses."

- **Not accepting mercy:** The second is if the son had rejected his father's forgiveness. He could have said, "Didn't you hear me? I said I don't deserve to be called your son, so just give me a job."

- **Not showing mercy:** The third is if the older son didn't forgive the younger. He didn't want to be in the same room as his brother, and so he was missing out on the party.

It is important to recognize that God does everything he can to let us know we are loved and to save us. It would be hard to image what more he could do.

Our Identity as His Child

You may have noticed that this lesson returned to our first Characteristic of a Disciple: Identity. We have already reflected on how we are sons and daughters of God. The main point for this lesson is that we will never be orphaned, never be disowned, never be rejected. Even if we walk away, the Father is always waiting with open arms, ready to forgive, and ready to celebrate our return.

JESUS I TRUST IN YOU!

5. What stood out to you in the reading?

6. Which do you struggle with the most: not asking for mercy, not accepting mercy, or not showing mercy?

FOR YOUR ✝ GATHERING

RECALL (20-30 minutes): Begin with the Scripture and the prayer from the Front Page of the week. Then the Quad shares with each other how their week was, with a particular emphasis on how they experienced God working in their life. How did everyone do on the "This Week I Will" challenge?

REFLECT (50-60 minutes): The Quad shares how he or she answered the six questions from the lesson, as well as any inspirations he or she received from "The Daily Bread" or their daily meditation on the main verse for the week.

RESOLVE (10-15 minutes): The facilitator says, "This week we read about how the mercy of God is far greater than our own. Ours is limited, his is limitless. Many of us spend a lot of time in prayer trying to convince God to forgive us. Little do we realize that the entirety of Scripture is focused on trying to convince *us* that there is no end to his mercy! God does not forgive us begrudgingly, as if he says, "Well, I'll forgive you this time as long as you don't do it again." We read in Luke 15 that there is more rejoicing over one sinner repenting than ninety-nine who were faithful. In fact, every story ends with a celebration. Reflecting on God's mercy is not a cause for guilt and condemnation, but rejoicing! Too often we live lives of 'Catholic guilt' when Jesus wants us to live in Catholic joy! **In light of that, what is one thing you can do this week to rejoice in God's mercy?**"

Discuss. Write down that resolution on the "This Week I Will" part of the Front Page of the following week. Then the Quad shares what else they would like prayer for and writes those intentions down in the space provided.

The facilitator then introduces the topic for the next week. Then he or she says, "Let us take a moment to listen to the living Word of God," and reads the accompanying Scripture, followed by a moment of silent reflection. The session closes with the Quad saying the prayer for the next week together, followed by an Our Father and a Hail Mary.

Next week has a bonus section, Discipleship in Action!

THIS WEEK I WILL

✝ PRAYER REQUESTS

WEEK 18

The Blessed Sacraments
Catholic Church
CHARACTERISTIC OF A DISCIPLE: **SACRAMENTS**

PASTOR
Fr. Francis
RETIRED PRIEST
Fr. Benedict
DEACON
Dcn. Laurence
BUSINESS MANAGER
Peter Faber
YOUTH MINISTRY
John Bosco
MUSIC MINISTRY
Cecelia Noheadia
SOUP KITCHEN
Teresa Kolkata

Into the Arms of Mercy

The sacrament of Reconciliation is a gift from God so we can experience his mercy in an intimate way.

"Jesus, Son of David, have mercy on me!"
– Luke 18:38

3 SACRAMENTS

Heavenly Father, we thank you for loving us so much that you sent your only Son for our savation. May we always rejoice in your mercy, just as you rejoice in our repentance.
Amen.

WEEK 18

THE *Daily* BREAD

The Ten Commandments: **Exodus 20:1-17**

What "Thou shalt not kill" means: **Matthew 5:21-26**

What "Thou shall not commit adultery" means: **Matthew 5:27-30**

Heavenly treasure vs. earthly treasure: **Matthew 6:19-24**

A psalm of repentance: **Psalm 51**

Main Verse for the Week: **Luke 18:38**

FAITH SEEKING UNDERSTANDING

When Jesus first appeared to the apostles after the resurrection, Scripture says, "He breathed on them and said to them, 'Receive the Holy Spirit. Whose sins you forgive are forgiven them, and whose sins you retain are retained'" (John 20:22-23). It is worth noting that this is among the first things Jesus did when he saw them after the resurrection. It was almost like he couldn't wait to share this power with them!

A Time for Mercy

The timing of this gift was important. Earlier in the gospel, there is a story about when Sts. James and John were so upset at a village that wouldn't listen to Jesus that they wanted to send fire upon it (Luke 9:51-56). You would *not* want people with that attitude in charge of what is forgiven or not! However, Sts. James, John, and the other apostles were in a very different place after Good Friday. They had run away from Jesus and left him to die. They were in need of his mercy. And so right after Jesus says, "Peace be with you" (the Hebrew word for peace, *shalom*, is also a gesture of forgiveness), he breathed the Holy Spirit and gave the authority of forgiving sins. It is this gospel reading that we hear on the Sunday after Easter, Divine Mercy Sunday.

Jesus wouldn't give the apostles the authority to do something that wasn't needed. He wanted them to be the foundation of the Church which is the "dispenser of the mysteries" (1 Corinthians 4:1), the vessel by which we receive his merciful love in the sacraments. Our sins not only wound our relationship with Jesus, but also the Body of Christ: "Reconciliation with the Church is inseparable from reconciliation with God" (*Catechism*, 1445).

Sacraments of Forgiveness

Last month, we examined the Church's teaching on sacraments. They are "efficacious signs of grace" (*Catechism*, 1131);

powerful and intimate encounters through which God pours his life into ours. They are not just *a* way of experiencing God, they are *the* way. Since mercy is at the heart of God's love for us, it would make sense that he would give us not just one, but two sacraments that are focused on experiencing his forgiveness (though it can be rightly argued that all sacraments, since they are encounters of God's divine love, are also encounters with his divine mercy).

The first place we are forgiven is in the sacrament of Baptism, which washes away all sin. Unbaptized adults who come into the Church never have to "confess" anything—Baptism is being reborn into a new life, and the old life is left behind. This sacrament is the most necessary, as it opens up the other sacraments to us.

Though we emerge from the waters of baptism without sin, we unfortunately don't stay that way. Like the prodigal son, we willfully walk away from the Father's house, doing what we know to be wrong. How might we return? For one cannot be baptized twice. That is why we need the second sacrament of forgiveness, the sacrament of Reconciliation.

From Burden to Blessing

That beautiful experience of the father embracing the lost son is captured in the sacrament of Reconciliation. The point of this is not to punish ourselves by going over our sins, like one might stick a dog's nose in its feces to teach it not to relieve itself on the carpet (not a recommended practice, by the way). It is so that, after speaking the worst of what we have done, we can hear the words, "I absolve you of all your sins." When the priest says those words, he is *in persona Christi*—in the person of Christ. Just as the bread and wine become the Body and Blood of Jesus in the Eucharist, those words of absolution become the words of Jesus himself.

Jesus wants to tell you in person that he forgives you. That is what this sacrament is about. It is not a burden; it is a blessing. It is an incredible gift!

INTO THE ARMS OF MERCY

The sacrament of Reconciliation is not about us, it is about him. It isn't about focusing on our sin but celebrating God's love, mercy, and his faithfulness. It is a recognition that, no matter what we have done or will do, God's mercy is more powerful than sin; God's love is more powerful than death.

He *wants* to forgive you and to have you experience his mercy in a deeper way in the sacrament of Reconciliation. Look at the cross. Why else do you think he went to all that trouble?

1. What struck you from this reading?

2. Briefly write about an experience of God's mercy you've had in the Sacrament of Reconciliation (or an experience of God's mercy at another time).

SCRIPTURE

At this point in the gospel, the scribes and Pharisees had decided that Jesus was too dangerous to keep around, for his teachings had swayed many people away from their influence. But how to kill him? The Jews were subject to Roman law, and only the Romans had the only authority that could take another's life. This is why the Jews brought Jesus before Pontius Pilate on Good Friday—it wouldn't have been legal for them to execute him themselves (those involved would likely have been killed for doing so). Roman law was problematic for the Jews, not only because they wanted Jesus dead, but also because there were sins that were supposed to be punishable by death that they could no longer enforce, such as committing adultery.

Then one of the Pharisees had the idea of literally "killing two birds with one stone." If they could get Jesus to say that an adulterous woman should be stoned, not only would she die, but Jesus would be executed for breaking Roman law. Or, if he "wimped out," the people would lose faith in him.

Of course, when Jesus was offered an option between A or B, he usually chose C: "none of the above."

Pray over **John 8:1-11**. Try using the method of *lectio divina* that you read about in Week 16.

Prepare: Take a moment before reading the scriptures to put yourself in the presence of God. Ask the Holy Spirit to come more deeply into your heart and to open your eyes in a new way to his Word.

Read: Slowly read through the passage. At some point, a word, phrase, or sentence will jump out at you.

Reflect: Read it again, allowing yourself to be drawn into those words. Don't overthink or go into "study mode." Focus on the part that drew your attention in the first reading.

Respond: Read it a third time and apply it to your life. Journaling can be a good exercise in this movement.

Rest: You are in the presence of God now. You've read his living Word. Take some time to rest in his love. When distractions come, turn your heart back to the Lord.

3. What inspired you from reading God's Word?

4. Reread this story from the woman's perspective. She had been "caught in the act," meaning some men rushed in and grabbed her, then dragged her out of that house to the most public area in Jerusalem, the temple courtyard. An angry mob was ready to kill her. Jesus saved her life that day in both body and soul. How would you respond to that kind of experience of mercy?

faith INTO life

The sacrament of Reconciliation is known by other names as well: Conversion, Penance, and Confession. They all emphasize different aspects of this beautiful sacrament of healing. Like the Liturgy, many Catholics receive Reconciliation but don't exactly know what it is about. The sacrament is more than just the time when one is before the priest in the confessional—there are things that need to happen before and after that moment as well.

Contrition

The first movement of grace is when the Holy Spirit lets us feel contrition for our sins. The Church defines contrition as "the sorrow of the soul and detestation for the sin committed, together with the resolution not to sin again" (*Catechism,* 1451). This contrition is considered "perfect" when the motivation is love of God (when the focus is on him), or "imperfect" when there are other motivations, such as a realization of the ugliness of sin or the fear of punishment (when the focus is on us).

Sin can dull our senses and tricks us into thinking that what is wrong is right. That is why it is so important that we examine our conscience on a daily basis and especially before receiving Reconciliation. A person with a broken bone is likely aware of that problem, but it is the unseen cancer that can be even more dangerous. Just like we put our body through CT scans and X-rays to see the problems beneath the skin, we need to continue to shine the light of the Gospel into those hidden areas of our lives to reveal sins of which we might not even be aware.

Remember the words of St. John Paul II: "Sin constitutes man's misery." The goal is not guilt and punishment, but healing and forgiveness. Examining your conscience can be a scary thing to do, because you suddenly realize there is more wrong with you than you'd like to admit!

Confession

Now that we are aware of our sins, whether they be venial or mortal, we bring them to the sacrament of Reconciliation. We should try to confess all the sins we remember and not intentionally hold anything back, for as St. Jerome said, "If the sick person is too ashamed to show his wound to the doctor, the medicine cannot heal what it does not know."

St. Augustine explained this beautifully:

> Whoever confesses his sins... is already working with God. God indicts your sins; if you also indict them, you are joined with God. Man and sinner are, so to speak, two realities: when you hear 'man'— this is what God has made; when you hear 'sinner' — this is what man himself has made. Destroy what you have made, so that God may save what he has made.... When you begin to abhor what you have made, it is then that your good works are beginning, since you are accusing yourself of your evil works. The beginning of good works is the confession of evil works. You do the truth and come to the light (*Catechism,* 1458).

Absolution and Penance

When the priest says the words of absolution, "I absolve you of all your sins," he is acting *in persona Christi*, the Person of Jesus Christ. It is Jesus himself who says those words to us. The same voice that spoke creation into existence now speaks the sin out of our soul. We are returned to the waters of our baptism. By his grace, we are without sin.

However, the journey isn't over: "Absolution takes away sin, but it does not remedy all the disorders sin has caused" (*Catechism,* 1459). The priest prescribes a penance, an action of some sort that can help us with the wounds that were caused by sin: "It can consist of prayer, an offering, works of mercy, service of neighbor, voluntary self-denial, sacrifices, and above all the patient acceptance of the cross we much bear" (*Catechism,* 1460). The purpose behind anything we are prescribed to do is to configure us more closely with Christ.

More than just healing wounds of the past, through the grace of the sacrament, "the sinner is made stronger" (*Catechism,* 1469) to live a holier life. Just as a doctor would give medicine specific to your illness, the sacrament of Reconciliation abundantly pours God's grace out into where we need it the most.

A Regular Part of Your Life

The Church requires the faithful to receive the sacrament of Reconciliation at least once a year. However, our bishops suggest we receive it once a month. Some popes were known to receive it every day!

Anyone who is married knows that there are two phrases that need to be spoken sincerely and often: "I love you" and "I'm sorry." Hopefully, one says the first more than the second! We can say, "I love you," to God in the Eucharist, and, "I'm sorry," to God in Reconciliation. Receive the Eucharist at least every week; receive Reconciliation at least every month. Examine your conscience on a daily basis so you can turn away from your misery and toward God's mercy. Allow the grace of the Holy Spirit to give you freedom and healing. And remember that God is more patient with you than you probably are with yourself.

He loves you! He won't give up on you. His love never fails.

5. What stood out to you in the reading?

6. What part does the sacrament of Reconciliation currently play in your spiritual life?

The next page has a bonus section, Discipleship in Action!

DISCIPLESHIP IN ACTION

Every evening, the Church encourages us to take a moment to reflect on our day and examine our conscience. How did we behave as a disciple of Jesus Christ? When did we fail in doing that? How might we do better tomorrow?

The Examen

St. Ignatius of Loyola created a five-step process that he called the Examen. He encouraged everyone to do this every evening. It can take anywhere from five to 15 minutes.

- **Give thanks.** Reflect on the day and be grateful for it. Thank God for the little things (a good meal, beautiful weather, a conversation with a friend) and the big things (hey, you're still alive!).
- **Ask for the Spirit.** Ask the Spirit to reveal the day to you through God's eyes. Where was he present? What was he calling you to do? Did you answer that call?
- **Recognize failures.** Maybe it was something we did, or maybe it was something we should have done. Perhaps we were more selfish than giving, or desired comfort over holiness.
- **Ask for forgiveness and healing.** God is bigger than our sins and weaknesses and rejoices in showing us mercy. Offer your faults to God.
- **Pray about tomorrow.** Think through what will happen tomorrow and how it can be different with God's grace and love at the center of your life.

The Ten Commandments

Another popular way of examining our conscience is to pray over the Ten Commandments. This is usually a longer process and a great preparation before receiving Reconciliation. There are many great resources that do this. The United States Conference of Catholic Bishops have a number of them on their website at **usccb.org**.

I find it helpful to write down the areas of sin that come up in that kind of examination. Then I bring that list when I go to reconciliation (because if I don't, I always forget something). Then when I'm done, I tear up the list and throw it away. Or, if I'm feeling dramatic, I burn it. Because the Lord has forgiven it all on the cross!

Mortal and Venial Sins

Not all sin is the same. Scripture makes a distinction between two kinds of sin, mortal and venial (1 John 5:16). The word "venial" comes from Latin and means "forgivable"—though it wounds our relationship with God, it does not sever it. "Mortal" sins are deadly (like a "mortal wound" that someone dies from). This is when a person rejects God by his or her actions in such a way that they no longer walk with God. The Church tells us that mortal sins have three elements to them:

- **Grave matter:** The action is of a serious nature (for example: blasphemy, murder, or adultery).

- **Full knowledge:** The person fully knows that what they are doing is wrong.

- **Deliberate consent:** The person makes this action freely—they aren't coerced by someone else or able to stop themselves (such as in the case of addiction).

In my marriage, if I said something sarcastic or insulting to my wife, that would be a venial sin. It is serious, but not serious enough to break the relationship, and could be healed with a simple but sincere apology. However, if I had an affair with another woman, that would be mortal. The relationship would be over—unless I was willing to make serious reparation for what I had done. It is worth noting that numerous venial sins can become mortal over time if they are not repented of. Were I always sarcastic and insulting to my wife, that could eventually end our relationship, as well.

Sacramental Forgiveness of Sins

Venial sins can be forgiven through personal prayer and going to Mass. However, Reconciliation is a beautiful way to specifically receive grace (and pastoral guidance) in those struggles.

Mortal sins require the sacrament of Reconciliation. This is one of the greatest blessings of this sacrament. Even if we completely walk away from our life of baptismal grace, we can come back to the Church through Reconciliation. One early Church father called it "the second plank [of salvation] after the shipwreck which is the loss of grace" (*Catechism,* 1446).

It is good to know there is *always* a way home, no matter how far one strays.

FOR YOUR ✠ GATHERING

RECALL (20-30 minutes): Begin with the Scripture and the prayer from the Front Page of the week. Then the Quad shares with each other how their week was, with a particular emphasis on how they experienced God working in their life. How did everyone do on the "This Week I Will" challenge?

REFLECT (50-60 minutes): The Quad shares how he or she answered the six questions from the lesson, as well as any inspirations he or she received from "The Daily Bread" or their daily meditation on the main verse for the week.

RESOLVE (10-15 minutes): The facilitator says, "In an earlier session, we reflected on the words of St. John Paul II: 'Mercy is an indispensable element of God's love. It is, as it were, love's second name.' God loves us through his mercy for us. It is what we most need and what he most wants to give. Though there are many ways to receive God's mercy, one of the most intimate and powerful ways is through the sacrament of Reconciliation. If only we would be as reluctant to sin as we often are to confess those sins! The sacrament of Reconciliation is more than acknowledging what we did in the past. It also gives us grace to heal those wounds and live a more holy life in the future. **What can you do this week to make the sacrament of Reconciliation a more active part of your spiritual life? When is the next time you intend to receive it?**"

Discuss. Some options could be to receive it more frequently, prepare for it more prayerfully, do more regular examinations of conscious, etc. One of the simplest resolutions would be, "I will go this Saturday." Write down those resolutions on the "This Week I Will" part of the Front Page of the following week. Then the Quad shares what else they would like prayer for and writes those intentions down in the space provided.

The facilitator then introduces the topic for the next week. Then he or she says, "Let us take a moment to listen to the living Word of God," and reads the accompanying Scripture, followed by a moment of silent reflection. The session closes with the Quad saying the prayer for the next week together, followed by an Our Father and a Hail Mary.

THIS WEEK I WILL

✝ PRAYER REQUESTS

WEEK 19

The Blessed Sacraments
Catholic Church

CHARACTERISTIC OF A DISCIPLE: SACRAMENTS

The Healing Power of Jesus

Jesus not only suffered for us, but he suffers with us, and through that suffering brings healing.

PASTOR
Fr. Francis

RETIRED PRIEST
Fr. Benedict

DEACON
Dcn. Laurence

BUSINESS MANAGER
Peter Faber

YOUTH MINISTRY
John Bosco

MUSIC MINISTRY
Cecelia Noheadia

SOUP KITCHEN
Teresa Kolkata

"Yet it was our pain that he bore, our sufferings he endured... by his wounds we were healed." – Isaiah 53:4-5

Jesus, you had the power to avoid suffering for yourself, yet you embraced a greater suffering than we could ever bear, and you did that out of love for us. Heal us through your wounds.
Amen.

3 SACRAMENTS

THE *Daily* BREAD

WEEK 19

Comfort in affliction: **2 Corinthians 1:3-7**

Cleansing of the leper: **Luke 5:12-16**

Lack of faith: **Mark 6:1-6**

Healing body and soul: **Mark 2:1-12**

Casting out demons: **Mark 5:1-13**

Main Verse for the Week: **Isaiah 53:4-5**

① ② ③ ④ ⑤ ⑥ ⑦

FAITH SEEKING UNDERSTANDING

Some disciples of John the Baptist came to Jesus to make sure he was the Messiah. Jesus replied by saying, "Go and tell John what you hear and see: the blind regain their sight, the lame walk, lepers are cleansed, the deaf hear, the dead are raised, and the poor have the good news proclaimed to them" (Matthew 11:4-5).

Jesus pointed to his healing miracles as proof that he was who he said he was. Throughout the gospels, we read many stories of Jesus healing people, both naturally and supernaturally.

Physical Healings

Jesus had only just called St. Peter and the other fishermen off the boat when a leper approached him. Those who had leprosy were outcasts from society. They had to live in their own communities. Whenever they approached others, they had to ring a bell and shout, "Unclean!" to warn anyone who might come near. The new followers of Jesus must have been shocked to see a leper so close.

The leper fell on the ground and said, "Lord, if you wish, you can make me clean" (Luke 5:12). Jesus *touched* the leper. Then he told him, "I do will it. Be made clean" (Luke 5:13). The man was cured!

There is a beautiful interaction here. First, the leper didn't doubt that Jesus had the power to heal, but he wondered if he wanted to. He made no demands; he just humbled himself before Jesus.

Second, Jesus touched the leper before healing him. He could have healed him from a distance, or he could have healed him first and touched him later. To touch a leper made one "unclean." Jesus was willing to enter into the leper's "uncleanness" before making him whole again. Finally, Jesus said, "I do will it"—he wanted the man to be healed. And so he was.

Jesus healed all kinds of sicknesses, and even raised people from the dead. However, there is one story in the gospels where miracles didn't occur. It was when he went home to visit Nazareth, but the townspeople wouldn't believe in him. "So he was not able to perform any mighty deed there, apart from curing a few sick people by laying his hands on them. He was amazed at their lack of faith" (Mark 6:5-6). Faith was an important part of being healed.

Spiritual Healings

Jesus not only healed bodies, but souls. He had only just begun his public ministry when a man possessed by a demon cried out, "What have you to do with us, Jesus of Nazareth? Have you come to destroy us?" (Mark 1:24). Jesus rebuked that demon and set the man free. This happened numerous times in the gospels. There was even a man who was possessed by numerous demons (Mark 5:1-20). In all of these instances, Jesus removed them with his command.

Another spiritual healing that Jesus did was the forgiveness of sin, as we examined last week. This was truly shocking! The Pharisees complained, "Who but God can forgive sins?" (Mark 2:7). They didn't realize that God was in their midst.

The most profound spiritual healings were the conversion of the hearts of those who came to believe in him. Fishermen left their nets, tax collectors left their booths, and even prostitutes left their way of life behind in order to follow in Jesus' footsteps.

Jesus Gave His Power to Others

Jesus did not want to keep this power to himself. In the ninth chapter of Luke, Jesus "gave [the Apostles] power and authority over all demons and to cure diseases, and he sent them to proclaim the kingdom of God and to heal the sick" (Luke 9:1-2). And that is what they did! This is one of the many moments where I wish we had more stories in the Gospels. I would love to read about what it was like for Simon the first time he cast out a demon, or for Andrew when he healed someone who was blind.

THE HEALING POWER OF JESUS

The healing ministry of Jesus, both naturally and supernaturally, didn't end with the apostles. It has continued on in the life of the Church. It is sacramentally present in the two sacraments of healing: Reconciliation (which cures the soul) and the Anointing of the Sick (which cures the body). It is present in the Church's authority to exorcise demons. It is present in the prayers of the Church, especially those offered at Mass, for the healing of those who are sick and the conversion of those who are lost.

WEEK 19

1. What struck you from this reading?

2. How have you experienced the healing power of Jesus in your life?

THE HEALING POWER OF JESUS

SCRIPTURE

The gospels tell numerous stories about two sisters who were close to Jesus, Mary and Martha. It was clear that Jesus loved them very much, so you can imagine their surprise when Jesus wasn't there when they felt they needed him most: **John 11:1-44**.

3. What inspired you from reading God's Word?

4. Why do you think Jesus allowed Lazarus to die before he healed him?

faith INTO life

I find the eleventh chapter of John to be one of the most beautiful stories in all of the gospels. There was no doubt that Jesus was going to heal Lazarus, for he told his disciples as much before he even left to go to Bethany. What is amazing is what transpires before he does it.

A God Who Enters into Our Suffering

"Jesus wept" (John 11:35). It is the shortest verse in the Bible but it speaks volumes about who Jesus is and how he wants to love us. Jesus had the power to heal. He had the desire to heal. He even said he was going to heal. And yet the God who became man became overwhelmed with grief and wept at the tomb of a friend. It is an image worth taking to prayer.

Jesus was like us in all things but sin. He not only took on human flesh, he took on human existence. The gospels tell stories of him rejoicing at the success of the apostles (Luke 10:21), exhausted from doing ministry (Mark 4:35-41), and agonizing in the garden (Luke 22:44). He experienced it all.

If I had the power that Jesus had, I confess I would likely "cheat" at life. If I got tired, I'd make myself more alert. If I was confused, I'd look into the future to find the right thing to do (or place the right bet!). If I, or someone I loved, was suffering, I'd take away the pain.

Martha and Mary were suffering. Jesus could have healed Lazarus from a distance, but he didn't. Instead, he walked a long journey to meet them in that place of suffering. He listened to how upset they were at him. He wept at the tomb. It tells us something profound about how God wants to encounter us.

Love, Not Power

In our moments of sickness, suffering, or death, our first response is to cry out to God so he will take away the pain. Sometimes he does. Sometimes he doesn't. Many argue that God can't exist because there is suffering in the world. How can a God who claims to be all-loving and all-powerful allow tragedy and hardship? He is either A) not all-powerful or all-loving, or B) isn't real. But as we've said before, when you give God options A and B, he usually goes with option C.

In this case, that surprising option is that God wants to enter into the very thing we are trying to avoid. He wants to weep with us there. We want to be emancipated from our pain; Jesus wants to embrace us in his wounds. We want him to display the heights of his power. He wants to show us the depths of his love.

The central image of our faith is an innocent man who died out of love for others. He who was like us in all things but sin bore all the sin of the world. He wants to transform our suffering into something sacred, just as he used an instrument of torture and death to become the pathway for eternal life.

The Temporary and the Eternal

Jesus rose Lazarus from the dead. But is Lazarus still with us today? No. He actually died (again), as did everyone that Jesus healed 2,000 years ago. This is because all physical healing is temporary. In fact, there are times in the Gospel when it seems that Jesus only healed the body to prove that he had power to heal the soul (Mark 2:1-12; it is one of your daily readings). It isn't that God isn't concerned with our bodies, but he is more concerned with our spiritual lives than our physical lives. He wants to use what we experience naturally to help us understand his supernatural power and love.

I know God's healing power is active today, both in the body and the soul. I have had answered prayers. I have experienced miracles in my own life and others. However, I have also experienced tragedies so deep that I was tempted to question the good things God had done in the past. When I realized that Jesus was weeping beside me in those dark moments, it brought healing to my heart.

"Who has known the mind of the Lord?" (Isaiah 40:13). We don't always understand what God is doing. Sometimes I have been challenged by those who are upset at the Lord to explain why bad things are happening. I can't. I'm not God.

But I know he exists. I know he loves us. I know he can transform suffering into salvation, death into life. This is not a "blind" faith, for I've seen plenty of miracles—the greatest of which is how my life has been changed by his love. And because of that I look forward to an even greater miracle: a sinner like me entering into the eternal love of God.

Hope for Healing

Scripture tells us that "all things work for good for those who love God" (Romans 8:28). We need to have hope in the midst of our suffering that something bigger is going on for the sake of our salvation or the salvation of others.

Like the leper we reflected on earlier, we need to fall down before the Lord and ask for healing while also being willing to accept his will. In the garden, Jesus prayed, "Father, if you are willing, take this cup away from me; still, not my will but yours be done" (Luke 22:42). Yes, even Jesus knows what it is like to have unanswered prayers!

> For we do not have a high priest who is unable to sympathize with our weaknesses, but one who has similarly been tested in every way, yet without sin. So let us confidently approach the throne of grace to receive mercy and to find grace for timely help (Hebrews 4:15-16).

Because Jesus knows what suffering is like, we should approach him with confidence. We should persevere in prayer. We should fast. We should bring our intentions to the Eucharist. If physical healing needs to be involved, we should receive the Anointing of the Sick (it isn't just for when you are about to die). This isn't like kicking a vending machine that didn't dispense the candy we paid for. It is offering up our suffering and the suffering of others so that we can encounter God's love in a more profound and intimate way.

Miracles will happen! God answers every prayer, though sometimes in ways we do not expect (or, at the time, don't want).

One of my favorite movie quotes is from the Princess Bride: "Life is pain, highness. Anyone who tells you differently is selling something." The world tries to "sell" a lot of different ways to avoid suffering, and some even suggest that if you follow Jesus, he will take all your suffering away. That isn't what the Bible says.

Our pain reminds us that this world is not our home. Heaven is described as a place where "[God] will wipe away every tear from their eyes, and there shall be no more death or mourning, wailing or pain" (Revelation 21:4). To bring us to heaven, God took on human flesh so we can be healed by his wounds. He does not promise to remove suffering. He transforms it, and in the process wants to transform us. For God "encourages us in our every affliction, so that we may be able to encourage those who are in any affliction with the encouragement with which we ourselves are encouraged by God" (2 Corinthians 1:4).

5. What stood out to you in the reading?

6. How have you experienced Jesus in the difficult moments of your life?

FOR YOUR ✝ GATHERING

RECALL (20-30 minutes): Begin with the Scripture and the prayer from the Front Page of the week. Then the Quad shares with each other how their week was, with a particular emphasis on how they experienced God working in their life. How did everyone do on the "This Week I Will" challenge?

REFLECT (50-60 minutes): The Quad shares how he or she answered the six questions from the lesson, as well as any inspirations he or she received from "The Daily Bread" or their daily meditation on the main verse for the week.

RESOLVE (10-15 minutes): The facilitator says, "Suffering, pain, and death are things of this world, brought on by the sin of humanity. Jesus experienced them all so that we might be healed, body and soul. We will fully experience this healing at the resurrection of the dead, when our bodies will be reunited with our souls in a glorified state (if we die before Jesus comes again). **If you are suffering physically, ask your priest this week for the Anointing of the Sick.** Sadly, many Catholics, even those who believe in the presence of Christ in the Eucharist, often discount his presence in the Anointing of the Sick. It is a powerful means of physical healing.

If you are suffering emotionally with a painful memory or experience, offer this to the Lord and ask for the prayers of others in your Quad. One of the best ways we can pray for the healing of the suffering of others is to take on little sufferings ourselves. This is known as fasting. **The Quad challenge this week (in addition to receiving the Anointing of the Sick if you need to, or at least scheduling a time to do so), is to share as much as you are comfortable something you are currently suffering with the other members of the Quad and do a small fast this week for their sufferings. If it is too painful or personal to share, just say, 'Please pray for a special intention.'"**

Discuss. The "small fast" could happen on one day of the week, such as giving up social media or a favorite drink (the Church encourages Friday as a day of fasting, which will be examined in a later topic). Or it might be something that lasts the whole week, like not listening to the radio on the way to work. There is no wrong way to do it, except to perhaps to overdo it! Keep it small, simple, and doable. Jesus is the healer, not you. Keep your prayer focused on him.

Write down those resolutions on the "This Week I Will" part of the Front Page of the following week. Then the Quad shares what else they would like prayer for and writes those intentions down in the space provided.

The facilitator then introduces the topic for the next week. Then he or she says, "Let us take a moment to listen to the living Word of God," and reads the accompanying Scripture, followed by a moment of silent reflection. The session closes with the Quad saying the prayer for the next week together, followed by an Our Father and a Hail Mary.

THIS WEEK I WILL >

✝ PRAYER REQUESTS

_____

_____

_____

_____

WEEK 20

COMMUNITY NEWS
CHARACTERISTIC OF A DISCIPLE: COMMUNITY

PART OF A BODY

It isn't about "me and Jesus" but "we and Jesus."

LIVING WORD

"For in one Spirit we were all baptized into one body."
– 1 Corinthians 12:13

COMMUNITY

Heavenly Father, you love each and every one of us with the same love you have for your Son. Through your Holy Spirit, may we love each other as you have loved us.
Amen.

THE *Daily* BREAD

WEEK 20

The early Christian community: **Acts 2:42-47**

Encouragement to use our gifts: **Romans 12:2-8**

Overcoming division: **1 Corinthians 3:1-23**

The importance of loving each other: **Romans 12:9-21**

The example of Jesus: **John 13:4-17**

Main Verse for the Week: **1 Corinthians 12:13**

① ② ③ ④ ⑤ ⑥ ⑦

FAITH SEEKING UNDERSTANDING

Many Catholics are surprised to discover that the Church celebrates her birthday not on Easter, but on Pentecost. Why? Because until then, the resurrection of Christ was a private event known only to a handful of followers. If you time-traveled back to the days after Jesus was crucified, you would have heard talk about a "false Messiah" who was killed and heard rumors of a missing body from the tomb. It wasn't until 50 days later when St. Peter, filled with the Holy Spirit, proclaimed to a crowd of thousands, "Therefore let the whole house of Israel know for certain that God has made him both Lord and Messiah, this Jesus whom you crucified" (Acts 2:36).

It says in Scripture that they were "cut to the heart" and asked, "What are we to do?" St. Peter replied, "Repent and be baptized, every one of you, in the name of Jesus Christ for the forgiveness of sins; and you will receive the Holy Spirit" (Acts 2:38). They did, and "about 3,000 persons were added that day" (Acts 2:41).

Baptized into a Community

Notice the choice of the words: 3,000 persons were *added* that day. Added to what? A *community*. This was the birth of the Church. Even though they had come to Jerusalem from around the Roman Empire, they all left their homes behind and moved so they could be together. Scripture described this first faith community: "All who believed were together and had all things in common; they would sell their property and possessions and divide them among all according to each one's need" (Acts 2:44, 45).

This was not promoting a godless social order, like communism (St. Paul told the early Christian community in 2 Thessalonians 3:10, "If anyone is unwilling to work, neither should that one eat"). It was about a group of people who were so moved by what Jesus had done for them that they stopped caring about their money and possessions and started caring about each other. They were willing to make sacrifices for each other because of what Jesus sacrificed for them. This is at the heart of what the Church is about.

Not "Me" and Jesus, But "We" and Jesus

The *Catechism* says, "Baptism makes us members of the Body of Christ: 'Therefore... we are members one of another'" (1267). We are not only bound to Jesus; we are also bound to each other as a family of God.

That is worth a moment of reflection. One cannot self-baptize. We enter in the faith through a community, and it is among the community that we are called to live it out. Though we certainly need our relationship with Jesus to be intimate and personal, it must also be communal.

St. John Chrysostom wrote:

> You cannot pray at home as at church, where there is a great multitude, where exclamations are cried out to God as from one great heart, and where there is something more: the union of minds, the accord of souls, the bond of charity, the prayers of the priests (*Catechism*, 2179).

A Part of a Family

Being Catholic isn't like being Republican or Democrat—people who agree on a certain political viewpoint. It isn't a "Jesus fan club" where we happen to admire the same person. Neither of those imply a responsibility to others.

In baptism, we not only received a Father (and a Mother in Mary—more on that later), but also brothers and sisters. Jesus told his apostles, "As I have loved you, so you also should love one another. This is how all will know that you are my disciples, if you have love for one another" (John 13:34-35). We show how much we love God by the love we have for each other.

PART OF A BODY

Unfortunately, our culture prizes (and even worships) individualism so much that many in the family of God act as if they are an only child. They behave like they are a member of an audience, not a member of the Body of Christ. They go to church like one would go to a play. Few realize that, as disciples of Jesus Christ, we don't *go* to church at all.

We *are* Church. We are the Body of Christ. We are the family of God.

The Front Page for Community gets its look from a bulletin board. Back in the days before social media, this is how you would find out what is going on in the community!

WEEK 20

1. What struck you from this reading?

2. What does it mean for you to read, "We are not only bound to Jesus; we are also bound to each other as a family of God?"

PART OF A BODY

SCRIPTURE

The Church in Corinth was, simply put, a mess. One of the biggest problems was divisions within the community of faith. So, St. Paul tried to use a simple analogy to show how they should be united: **1 Corinthians 12:4-13:13**.

3. What inspired you from reading God's Word?

4. What quality of love do you find to be the biggest challenge?

faith INTO life

Although your reading was from two different chapters, and those who published the Bible you read might have inserted a few different headings, it all makes the same point: we have to be united in love.

"Love" is a powerful word and can mean different things to different people. So, St. Paul made it clear. The love that he wrote about wasn't just emotional or romantic. It was patient and kind. It rejoiced with the truth. It bore, believed, hoped, and endured all things. It never failed. St. Paul also told us what love was not: jealous, pompous, inflated, rude, selfish, or quick-tempered. It did not rejoice in wrongdoing nor hold a grudge.

St. Paul gave the Church in Corinth—and us—a checklist to see how well we are doing in our love for one another. Are we patient or are we quick-tempered? Are we kind or are we rude? Do we have a love that can endure all things, like people we don't like, music we don't enjoy, or a homily that goes too long? Or even more serious things, like scandal within the Church (for "if one part suffers, all the parts suffer with it")? Whatever our function within the Body of Christ, love is the goal. And if we do our part without loving, it means nothing.

"We," Not "Us" and "Them"

One of the biggest obstacles in loving each other is division. Even with other Catholics, we are tempted to divide between "us" and "them." The most diabolical (literally, "of the devil") division can happen over the way we celebrate the Mass. As Fr. Dave Pivonka, the current president of Franciscan University of Steubenville, once said, "The devil would have us the most divided at the place where we are supposed to be the most united."

Jesus was known as the "friend of sinners" (Matthew 11:19); the devil was known as the "accuser of brothers" (Revelation 12:10). It isn't that we can't disagree with each other (every family does) but the most important thing is how we love each other in the midst of those disagreements, even with those we would consider "our enemies" (Matthew 5:44).

This kind of supernatural love is not something we can create on our own. It is a gift of the Holy Spirit that we received in baptism, for "God is love" (1 John 4:12). We need to keep asking God for this gift in our prayer.

Overcoming Our Pride

In the family of God, we don't want to behave as spoiled children who think it is all about them. In today's culture, we can become very protective of our rights but negligent about our duties—and even fail to see a connection between the two. Baptism is a gift, but also an obligation:

> Having become a member of the Church, the person baptized belongs no longer to himself, but to him who died and rose for us. From now on, he is called to be subject to others, to serve them in the communion of the Church, and to 'obey and submit' to the Church's leaders, holding them in respect and affection (*Catechism*, 1269).

Because the greatest of all virtues is love, one might think the greatest sin would be hate. Actually, it is pride. Our pride rebels at phrases such as "subject to others" and "obey and submit." Pride is a love of self before others, whereas the love that Jesus modeled was a love of others before ourselves. Jesus made himself subject to the Roman authorities that crucified him and submitted to the will of the Father, even to his death. He did this all for us. Like the first Christian community, we should be moved to sacrifice for each other because of what Jesus sacrificed for us.

From Local to Global

Before Jesus ascended into heaven, Jesus told the apostles, "You will receive power when the Holy Spirit comes on you, and you will be my witnesses in Jerusalem, throughout Judea and Samaria, and to the ends of the earth" (Acts 1:8). They were in Jerusalem at the time. Judea and Samaria were the next regions. The "ends of the earth" were beyond those. His message to the apostles was to start locally and then move globally. That is a good model for us, as well.

For many of us, the first place we need to build community is our family, the "domestic Church." Do we respect our parents? How can we love our spouses better (if you have one)? What is more important to us, success at work or having a loving relationship with our children?

From there, we should look at our local parish. Do we participate in anything other than Mass? Do we volunteer for things? Do we financially support our parish and diocese?

Beyond that, there might be other ministries in the local area, country, or even other countries that we feel called to support or be a part of. Have we taken time to consider what those might be?

It is important that we keep these priorities in mind. It wouldn't be right to be financially generous to a national ministry but completely neglect the local parish. Just as it wouldn't be right to spend so much time doing ministry at your parish that you neglect the needs of your family.

From Consumer to Servant

To change a famous phrase, we need to "ask not what the Church can do for us, but what we can do for the Church." We need to ask the Spirit to move our hearts (not just our own, but everyone in our faith community) from a consumer mentality to a servant spirituality. The more we humble ourselves in service to each other, the more deeply we encounter Christ.

The challenge is not just to "do more things," but to do these things with the love about which St. Paul wrote. In my own life, I must confess there were times I served the Church not out of love, but out of pride. I thought I was better than others because of my service. At other times, I got angry at others because they didn't work as hard as I did. It is an easy trap to fall into.

You might have many reasons why you don't want to participate in your local parish or diocese, but remember that the love that God gives us "endures all things." You are a member of this body, a part of this family. You'll be surprised how one person—or even four—can change the dynamic of a faith community when they offer themselves in love for others.

PART OF A BODY

5. What stood out to you in the reading?

6. Is there division in your faith community, and, if so, how can you help heal it?

FOR YOUR ✝ GATHERING

RECALL (20-30 minutes): Begin with the Scripture and the prayer from the Front Page of the week. Then the Quad shares with each other how their week was, with a particular emphasis on how they experienced God working in their life. How did everyone do on the "This Week I Will" challenge?

REFLECT (50-60 minutes): The Quad shares how he or she answered the six questions from the lesson, as well as any inspirations he or she received from "The Daily Bread" or their daily meditation on the main verse for the week.

RESOLVE (10-15 minutes): The facilitator says, "Our pride puts the focus on ourselves. The love of God puts the focus on others. The lie of sin tells us we will be happiest if we focus on ourselves. The truth of Jesus reveals that, 'For whoever wishes to save his life will lose it, but whoever loses his life for my sake will find it' (Matthew 16:25). Just as a part of a body is only understood in the context of the whole, so we as a body of Christ can only find our happiness and purpose in the context of community. That begins within our families and then extends to our parishes (our "family of faith") and the wider community in which we live. We can be tempted to take a passive role in those communities, judging their value based on what they can do for "me." The challenge this week is to be more active, more focused on "we." **This week, what is one thing you can do to strengthen a community that you are a part of (family, parish, work, etc.) and more actively love others within them?**

Discuss. Write down that resolution on the "This Week I Will" part of the Front Page of the following week. Then the Quad shares what else they would like prayer for and writes those intentions down in the space provided.

The facilitator then introduces the topic for the next week. Then he or she says, "Let us take a moment to listen to the living Word of God," and reads the accompanying Scripture, followed by a moment of silent reflection. The session closes with the Quad saying the prayer for the next week together, followed by an Our Father and a Hail Mary.

Looking ahead: Guidebook, Part III will be needed soon!

THIS WEEK I WILL >

✝ PRAYER REQUESTS

WEEK 21

COMMUNITY NEWS
CHARACTERISTIC OF A DISCIPLE: COMMUNITY

"AND THEY WERE ALL OF ONE HEART..."

Unity takes humility, grace, and a lot of work.

LIVING WORD
"I pray...that they may all be one, as you, Father, are in me and I in you, that they also may be in us, that the world may believe that you sent me."
—John 17:20-21

5 COMMUNITY

Most Holy Trinity, you are a community of life-giving love. Heal the wounds of division among us and inspire us to reflect the love you have in yourself by the way we love each other.
Amen.

WEEK 21

THE *Daily* BREAD

The humble example of Christ: **Philippians 2:1-11**

Love, the bond of perfection: **Colossians 3:12-17**

How good it is!: **Psalm 133**

The importance of mutual affection: **Romans 12:9-21**

The prayer of Jesus: **John 17:20-26**

Main Verse for the Week: **John 17:20-21**

"AND THEY WERE ALL OF ONE HEART..."

FAITH SEEKING UNDERSTANDING

"The community of believers was of one heart and mind," is how the book of Acts describes the earliest followers of Jesus (Acts 4:32). Unfortunately, it didn't stay that way. The next story was about how two people in the community lied about the money they donated. A few chapters later, the Lord revealed to St. Peter that Gentiles (non-Jews) can also be baptized, and that caused a lot more confusion and division. (The earliest followers of Jesus were all Jewish. They weren't called "Christians" until Gentiles joined the faith.)

The Importance of Unity

Not surprisingly, Jesus saw this coming. His final words before he was arrested was a prayer to the Father for unity of the believers:

> I pray not only for them [the apostles], but also for those who will believe in me through their word, so that they may all be one, as you, Father, are in me and I in you, that they also may be in us, that the world may believe that you sent me. And I have given them the glory you gave me, so that they may be one, as we are one, I in them and you in me, that they may be brought to perfection as one, that the world may know that you sent me, and that you loved them even as you loved me (John 17:20-24).

I love this Scripture. He was praying for us, we who believe in him because of the teaching of the apostles! He had all of us in mind before he headed to his suffering and death.

What was he worried about? That we wouldn't be united. He said when we are one, "the world may believe that you sent me." When we are united we show that Jesus was sent by the Father. Unfortunately, the opposite is also true. When we are divided, it makes Jesus' message less credible. How can we claim to love God if we can't love each other?

A Broken Body of Christ

Unfortunately, there are many divisions within Christianity today. There are thousands of Christian denominations within the United States alone, and "fighting/disagreements among Christians" is often listed as one of the top reasons why non-believers aren't interested in Christ.

For the first thousand years, the Church was one. Then, in 1054, the Eastern and Western Church broke apart. Those from the East became known as "Orthodox" (or "Eastern Orthodox") and the Western Church became known as "Latin." One of the reasons for this split was over who had authority. The Latin Church believed it should be the chair of Peter (the pope in Rome), while the Orthodox believed it should be the patriarch in Constantinople (which was the capital of the empire at the time).

In the 16th century, more divisions occurred. "Authority" was once again a significant factor. Those in England believed the king should have religious authority, and they became Anglicans. Some in Europe believed the Bible should be the only authority, and they became Protestants. There were as many different groups of Protestants as there were different interpretations of the Bible: Lutherans, Calvinists, etc.

A Catholic Perspective

The divisions between these beliefs can be so drastic that some think of them as different religions or different faiths. However, it is worth understanding our Catholic perspective on these divisions.

Christ has only one Body. We don't consider Catholicism to be one denomination of Christianity among many. In fact, we prefer to not think of other Christians as different "denominations" at all. We believe the fullness of the faith subsists in being Catholic, a word that means "universal." This is the universal Church of which all Christians are a part.

It might sound crazy, but we consider anyone who has been baptized, even if it didn't happen in a Catholic church, to be part of the Catholic faith. Because there is only one faith. In fact, if someone who was baptized in another Christian church wants to become Catholic through the RCIA process, we don't refer to him or her as a "catechumen" but as a "candidate for continuing conversion." They are already in the faith, they are just continuing the journey to the fullness of what God has revealed.

What do we mean by "fullness"? It is the apostolic succession that gave the pope and Magisterium their authority. It is all the books of the Bible. It is all seven sacraments. It is the heritage of faith passed down through the apostles and the saints. Some groups of Christians don't accept papal authority, some don't celebrate all the sacraments, others don't recognize some of the books of Scripture as inspired. This doesn't mean that there isn't grace and truth among those Christians, nor does it mean that the Holy Spirit isn't present. The Holy Spirit is present in all of us who proclaim "Jesus as Lord," and is at work trying to bring the body of Christ to the unity for which Jesus himself prayed.

Answering Christ's Prayer

The issues that divided followers of Jesus were not merely doctrinal. There were other political and historical things at work, and often both sides were to blame for the divisions that occurred. Misunderstandings and mistrust still exist today. Sadly, one need not look to other groups of Christians to see division; it often happens within our own Catholic dioceses and parishes.

Origen, an early father of the Church, rightly points out that at the heart of our divisions is sin: "Where there are sins, there are also divisions, schism, heresies, and disputes. Where there is virtue, however, there also are harmony and unity, from which arise the one heart and one soul of all believers" (*Catechism*, 817).

I hate it when my kids fight. I think my children don't realize how much it hurts me when they do. Unfortunately, I don't think that many Christians realize how our divisions hurt God our Father. Jesus prayed that we would all be one. It is time we took that prayer seriously and do what we can to answer that prayer by our love for one another.

The *Catechism* states:

> Christ always gives his Church the gift of unity, but the Church must always pray and work to maintain, reinforce, and perfect the unity that Christ wills for her. This is why Jesus himself prayed at the hour of his Passion, and does not cease praying to his Father, for the unity of his disciples (820).

"AND THEY WERE ALL OF ONE HEART..."

1. What struck you from this reading?

2. In your own words, why is unity among Christians so important?

SCRIPTURE

St. Paul frequently wrote about the importance of unity. In this reading, he not only explains why it is important but what we need to do to achieve it: **Ephesians 4:1-32**.

3. What inspired you from reading God's Word?

4. What did you find most challenging about this Scripture?

faith INTO life

St. Paul wrote similar things in other letters. At times, he was so passionate about unity it sounded like he was begging!

> If there is any encouragement in Christ, any solace in love, and participation in the Spirit, any compassion and mercy, complete my joy by being of the same mind, with the same love, united in heart, thinking one thing (Philippians 2:1-2).

There are a number of themes that emerge from St. Paul's writing that can help us be more united with each other.

Work for It

St. Paul told the Ephesians to "strive to preserve the unity of the spirit". Because of our sinfulness and selfishness, unity doesn't happen by default. Maybe we can find a small group of people who think like we think and like what we like. But it would be harder to find a larger group of such people, and impossible to find a church full of them.

Being a part of a community takes work. We have to ask the Spirit to change any attitude within our heart that tells us the Church is "mine" but not "ours." We should be willing to change the way we do things in order to accommodate others. Sometimes we can be too "democratic"— we follow the way of the majority, not the way of love.

Jesus worked hard for our unity, for he "broke down the dividing wall of enmity through his flesh" (Ephesians 2:14). His love shown on the cross both empowers and encourages us to love each other, even when it gets uncomfortable and difficult.

Embrace Diversity

St. Paul frequently used an analogy of a body with different parts when he spoke of the followers of Jesus. We are not all the same.

We have different gifts. We have different passions. A body made up entirely out of hands would not be very helpful!

We also have different backgrounds and perspectives. The *Catechism* states:

> Within the unity of the people of God, a multiplicity of peoples and cultures is gathered together. Among the Church's members, there are different gifts, offices, conditions, and ways of life… the great richness of such diversity is not opposed to the Church's unity (814).

The Catholic Church is the most diverse group of people on the planet! Our human nature often has us gravitate toward people who look and think like we do. If we let that happen, we would miss out on all that God wants us to experience.

Tangible Expressions of Love

St. Paul always accompanied his pleas for unity with a list of behaviors that were necessary to make it happen: kindness, gentleness, compassion, and humility. We have to be able to speak the truth to each other in a loving way when we disagree (Ephesians 5:25). That implies we should also humbly *listen* to the truth when it is spoken to us.

St. Paul writes we need to do all of this, "bearing with one another and forgiving each other, if one has a grievance against another; as the Lord has forgiven you, so you also must do" (Colossians 3:13). Families cannot survive without forgiveness. The more time we spend with others, the more likely we will do something that might hurt them, either intentionally or unintentionally. We will also get hurt. When that happens to me, I try not to assume the other person's motive towards me was hostile. It all goes back to love. "Over all these put on love, that is, the bond of perfection" (Colossians 3:14).

These behaviors, which are fruits of the Holy Spirit in our lives, turn a group of individuals into a *community*. Jesus wasn't looking to recruit members for an organization, but children for his family. The more we love each other, the more he can be at work in our lives.

Love with a Mission

Christians should love differently than the world does. We should stand out at work or at school. We should be caring for people that others don't. I remember my youth minister telling me, "The goal of Christianity is to love the unlovable person." That thought always challenged me. For, as Jesus said, "If you love those who love you, what credit is that to you? Even sinners love those who love them" (Luke 6:32).

This is the kind of love that sets us apart. "This is how all will know that you are my disciples, if you have love for one another" (John 13:35). The real question is, do we care if people know we are his disciples or not?

This faith is not a treasure that we are to keep for ourselves. It is meant to be shared with others. There are so many who do not know the love and mercy of Jesus Christ. The Father wants to bring more orphans into his family, just as he did with us. Before we can speak the "good news," we have to live it.

Jesus prayed for the unity of his disciples so the world would know that he was the Savior of the world. Let us continue to pray that prayer of Jesus and, empowered by the Spirit, share his love with our family, our places of work and school, our parish, and our world.

5. What stood out to you in the reading?

6. What behaviors of love do you think you can do better?

Bring Guidebook, Part Three to the next Q gathering!

"AND THEY WERE ALL OF ONE HEART..."

FOR YOUR ✝ GATHERING

RECALL (20-30 minutes): Begin with the Scripture and the prayer from the Front Page of the week. Then the Quad shares with each other how their week was, with a particular emphasis on how they experienced God working in their life. How did everyone do on the "This Week I Will" challenge?

REFLECT (50-60 minutes): The Quad shares how he or she answered the six questions from the lesson, as well as any inspirations he or she received from "The Daily Bread" or their daily meditation on the main verse for the week.

RESOLVE (10-15 minutes): The facilitator says, "Divisions with followers of Christ, whether they be divisions among Catholics or divisions between Christians in general, diminish the ability for the world to recognize Jesus as sent by our Father. In our previous topic, we read that Jesus was known as the 'friend of sinners' (Matthew 11:19) but the devil was known as the 'accuser of brothers' (Revelation 12:10). This isn't to say we can't disagree, but just that we don't define each other on what we disagree upon. More often than not, there is more that unites us than divides, but we have to work at establishing those bonds on unity. **As you consider the communities that you are a part of (family, parish, work, etc.), what is one thing you can do this week to be a source of unity?**

Discuss. Write down that resolution on the "This Week I Will" part of the Front Page of the following week (found in *The Discipleship Quad Guidebook, Part Three*). Then the Quad shares what else they would like prayer for and writes those intentions down in the space provided.

The facilitator then introduces the topic for the next week. Then he or she says, "Let us take a moment to listen to the living Word of God," and reads the accompanying Scripture, followed by a moment of silent reflection. The session closes with the Quad saying the prayer for the next week together, followed by an Our Father and a Hail Mary.

Looking Ahead

Before you go, look at the Facilitation Schedule at the beginning of *The Discipleship Quad Guidebook, Part Three*, and make sure that the members of the Quad know which upcoming Gatherings they will facilitate.

About the Author

Bob Rice loves being Catholic. He is a husband, father of seven, permanent deacon for the diocese of Steubenville, and Professor of Catechetics at Franciscan University of Steubenville. He has a PhD in Theology from Liverpool Hope University where he researched Catholic youth and evangelization. Deacon Bob is a highly sought after presenter at parish missions, youth conferences, men's conferences, young-adult gatherings, and catechetical workshops. He has authored many books and articles, including the *Discipleship Quad Guidebooks*, and a novel about St. Peter titled, *Between the Savior and the Sea*. He is the co-host of a popular weekly podcast called *They That Hope* with Fr. Dave Pivonka, TOR. Bob has recorded numerous albums (his music can be found on Apple Music, Spotify, and others) and leads worship for over ten thousand people every year, mostly through the Steubenville Adult Conferences. You can find out more about him at deaconbobrice.com.

Want to Listen to a Good Podcast?

They That Hope is a podcast with Fr. Dave Pivonka, TOR, and Bob Rice. They are two friends who see humor and hope in a crazy world. Each week, Fr. Dave and Bob invite the listener into their friendship as they talk about things going on in their lives and in the world—sports, culture, the Church, news, etc.—always trying to discover the presence of God and the hope of Jesus Christ in the midst of it. Each episode is between thirty and forty minutes and new episodes are available every Wednesday morning, both in audio and in video. Find out more at deaconbobrice.com.

Made in United States
Troutdale, OR
10/10/2023